Whispers

By Jonathan Russell

Shuffling through the Fall of sleep,
fond dreams begin to whisper

© copyright 2008, 2011 by Jonathan Russell
All Rights Reserved.

ISBN13: 978-1-931807-97-5

Library of Congress Control Number: 2011940432

Peter E. Randall Publisher LLC
Box 4726, Portsmouth NH 03802
www.perpublisher.com

Book design: Grace Peirce
www.nhmuse.com

Once There Was Only One won $1000 First Prize, 1998, American Poetry Association.

When the Milklight Breaks won $1000 First Prize, 1999, American Poetry Association.

To Shirley

A few of these poems have appeared in the literary journals of the following universities:

    Stephen Austin State University, Texas
    Sonoma State University, California
    Purdue University, Indiana
    University of Alaska, Juneau
    Southern Illinois University, Edwardsville
    Schoolcraft College, Livonia, Michigan

This mole of poetry in the dim light of his tunnel, is deeply grateful to Deidre Randall for her invaluable help and encouragement, and to Grace Peirce and Ann Downey at Peter E. Randall Publisher.

And to the following for their kindness in correcting a purblind mole's inevitable only too numerous tiresome typos: Melissa Barrett, Roberto Tirado, Caroline Russell-Smith, Cecilia Russell, Shari Belove, Giselle Wolf, Morley Jewell.

Also by Jonathan Russell

The Sea Cries Over My Shoulder
The Daisy Chain
Barking Down the Wind
Follow Me, David!
When Eyes Meet Over the Minestrone

Awards

1995, "International Literary Man of the Year for Services to Poetry," from the International Biographical Center, Cambridge, England

1993, Honorary Professor of Humanities at the Institute of Higher Economic and Social Studies, Brussels, Belgium

1993, Docteur des Lettres, Psychologie et Litterature, Academie des Sciences Humaines Universelle, Paris

1993, Honorary Doctorate in Literature, London Institute for Applied Research

1998, First Prize, American Poetry Association

1999, First Prize, American Poetry Association

Acknowledgments

BBC Radio, U.K., 1979, for: 'Oonala and the White Ants Sleeping', 'A Hole in the Darkness', 'Nature's Travelling Gentlemen'. Long Island, New York television, Lively Arts, 1989, for 'Sea Peace'. Lookout, magazine of Seamen's Church Institute, New York, 1987, for 'Great Call of the Sea'. New Voices in American Poetry, hardback anthology,1987, for 'Shadow'. American Poetry Association Anthology, 1988, for 'Once There Was Only One'. Re Arts and Letters, Stephen Austin State University, Texas, Spring, 1990, for 'When the Milklight Breaks'. Aim, magazine, Chicago, Fall 1988, for 'Equal Under the Moon'. Skylark, Purdue University, Indiana,1993, for 'Dearest, Did You Hear?'.

Dr. Jonathan Russell's poetry has earned him awards and recognition in England and in America, where he now lives as a naturalized American citizen.

His poems have appeared in journals of the Stephen Austin State University, Texas, Sonoma State University. California, Purdue University, Indiana, University of Alaska, Juneau, Southern Illinois University Edwardsville, and School-craft College, Livonia, MI.

Whispers is a collection of poems that celebrates love and the natural world, while they offer a profound reverance for life. At times uplifting and at times humorous, this volume will draw the reader into Russell's lush world of rich imagery.

As a poet, novelist, academic, and composer, Russell offers a unique viewpoint, as he is legally blind, yet "sees" perhaps with more clarity than those with sight.

Contents

- vii   Acknowledgments
- 1   The Love That Passed Us By
- 2   Whispers Over Our Shoulders
- 3   By the Sea of Crabs and Crocuses
- 4   The Richest Corpse in History
- 5   Equal Under the Moon
- 6   Ghost Ship
- 8   Once There Was Only One
- 9   The Army of the Dead
- 10   If Only
- 11   The Glowworm's Honeymoon.
- 12   Oonala and the White Ants Sleeping
- 22   The Miller's Daughter
- 23   Never Too Late for Love's Lottery
- 24   None Wiser Than the Foolish Heart
- 25   The Soul's Laundromat
- 26   The Riddle of the Middle Sex
- 27   Holy Holocaust
- 28   When the Moonlight Breaks
- 41   A Hole in the Darkness
- 43   Echoes
- 44   The Last Waltz
- 48   Poetry
- 49   Going Global
- 50   Great Call of the Sea
- 52   The Captain's Spirit
- 55   Endless Horizons
- 56   Trees
- 57   Nature's Traveling Gentlemen

59	Beyond Comparison
60	No Second Spring (the toxic truth)
61	A Day to be Free
66	Fateful Attraction!
67	The Beef and Pasta of Art
72	Delicate Vision!
73	To an Anonymous Lover
74	Sparrows of Paradise
77	The Drifter
89	Autumn Twilight
90	Box Car Barney
91	Sea Peace
93	Portrait of a Kiss
95	The Miracle
101	Prudence Primm
102	The Sadness of Green
103	The Spanish Crabs' Tarantelle
105	Sad Ladies of the Shells
106	Tinkles to Drizzle
107	Coffin in the Wind
108	Brother Rubberneck
111	The Pale Side of a Shadow
112	Through a Glass Staircase
118	Cucumber-young
121	Eden Without Eve
122	Dearest, Did You Hear?
126	Admiral Bembo
127	The Olympic Flame of Misconception
128	Valhalla Hill
137	Footprints in the Fog
138	Love in Winter is Summer in Disguise

139	Down the Crooked Path
140	Artemis in Acapulco
143	A Salt Water Mystery
145	Sleeping Dolphin
146	Barking to the Heart
148	Only Love Can Hold a Candle to the Moon
149	Whispers into Darkness
150	Apollo in a Pink Mirror
151	Death of a Smile
152	In Another Life
159	Sleeping Swan
160	Paws in Paradise
161	Cat Worship
162	The Older We Grow
163	Shipwrecked Mariners of the Heart
164	The River of Love
165	His Master's Voice
168	Child of Heaven
170	Shadow

The Love That Passed Us By

Fallen riders from the carousel of dreamers,
tumbled, humbled—hurled by make-believe,
be our own phoenixes—rise to splendorous life
—the love that passed us by! Too late we learn
that rainbows fade from showers of the eyes.
The Future is uncertain, so let it wishfully seem
again the echo of Spring calling from a cloud.
To hope is to wait for sun to snow on the blossom,
while never was it fairer than a lost sighing bosom.
O for that travel agency of last chances
—foreign lands while holding hands, for the lonely
hearts—but lucky horseshoes hesitate to knock!
Be bold, hold not onto the glut of the gloom.
Melting is the melon of the moon—borrow a star
from the night's tiara and put the sapphires of eyes
and the rubies of lips on our amor's shopping list,
as we encounter behind a counter Morpheus' beautiful
florist, watering her violets with tears of remorse
stained with mascara—so we ask for passion flowers.
And surprise! She wraps our nigellas in her hearts
    desire
—O what trysts to keep with our love-in-the-mist!
She lives solely in our imaginations—but no harm
in linking arms to the bus stop, not withstanding
truly we knew she'd vanish in the queue! As all
is not lost, when anon, we losers awake to an ache
—for the shine in her eyes casts her shadow to follow.

Whispers Over Our Shoulders

We fly in dreams, some as that bouncing girl
in the gym we once had been, others as that whistler
chasing the girl gazelle in micro skirts,
with her eyes grazing the lick of his lollipop
to share. Haunted by ghost of luscious lips,
he never grew up—Peter Pan
with a touch of arthritis, traipsing much mellowed
trendy Wendy—a nostalgic baby doll
shop-soiled but shampooed to everlasting
youth a trifle gray at the roots. Dreaming,
we return to the erstwhile elves of our selves
before the nuptial rigor mortis set in.
Melting memories lick our lollipops
still sticky on lover's lips that Time has kissed.

By the Sea of Crabs and Crocuses

In Bangor Wales, where I was born
the sun came up to show its smile
between the frowning roving clouds,
but before night fell it rained again
upon the walking shells and toddler I
paddling in the surf of spindrift brine.
The days were always happy holidays
as if summer had arrived to make us glad
—till the years slipped by to cloak my eyes.
We leapfrogged over the sadder times
in our magic world of make-believe.
The horizon woke up from the waves at dawn
to paint the crocuses purple on our lawn,
seeded to conform to a lover's moon
to delight the cuckoo and fools like I
who walked with crabs, treading the vines
of the shore's champagne popping grapes.
And tipsily I returned with the lisping tide
unsteady on toes and pale with pail
providing free transport for my friends
the crabs to come rolling home to tea with me.

The Richest Corpse in History

Not in state, it lies, in Paris' Père La Chaise,
with Sebastian Melmoth, and recognized celebrates.
No, the remains are hidden in a minuscule oubliette
with the unknown forgotten phoenixes of their bones.
Poignantly, two penurious untended plots
dotted with daisies and the weeds of memories,
plus a few immortalized by glazed photographs
—ghosts of the departed materializing marbleized.
The local exodus to the Promised Land simplified
in the case of the beloved brothers Van Gogh
—no monochromes, just gravestones—side
by side like fork and knife, at the feast of the missing
guests—arriving with wine and flowers of hindsight
from Art's unreliable celebrity florist in Posterity!

Equal Under the Moon

For every pair of lips that kisses,
another is being kissed goodbye;
for every marriage made in Heaven,
eleven are kissed from Paradise.
For every gorging glutton for mutton,
millions without rice for a skeleton;
for every tongue the grape intoxicates,
myriads from drought hallucinate.
For every aspirant put up for promotion,
another dispirited put down on the street;
for every foot treading red carpet,
countless treading the gutter.
For every soul traveling for pleasure,
thousands fleeing for their lives;
for every arm waving a banner,
another throwing a bomb;
for every soldier honored by medal,
legions honored by memorial.
All are equal under the moon,
but some are unequal under the sun.

Ghost Ship

Our telescopes we focus on a very strange
ship distantly ghosting veils of mist
—her ratlin's spider's webs to towering masts,
their crows' nests thread. Her billowing canvas
is spread to a doldrums' fading breath! The sea is
on its death bed. Eerily, we hear the vessel's
phantom bell pulled by its Turk's head,
by invisible hand summoning the unseen
    to the unheard.
We strain to descry: no speck of life
    on deck!
Where is her captain, bo's'n, or a few of the crew?
The fighting frigate is manned sans hands,
none on the helm, overwhelmed by fate unknown.
—

Yet mysteriously, she flies without wind,
as if driven by storm, rolling to the hornpipe
of its dervishes of spindrift. In an instant in the infinite
vagueness of distance faintly, but distinctly, we (imaging)
hear in our minds' horrified psychic ears
her exposed side explode in sundering thunder
of timber! Our vision blurs on the swirling veils
of mist, now turned to a blinding crimson. Wherein,
as flotsam she vanishes, sucked into a whirling
    all-swallowing vortex!
—

We refocus on the horizon's liquid oblivion
    —and a shrieking

fluttering of gulls soars therefrom
    reminding us
of an old sea legend we sailors inherit:
'they be the soaring of the drowned mariners'
    spirits!'
—

Long, we peer at the mirage—or lighting
    of truth(?)
by which our eyes and minds are opened wide
—as the bygone, fighting frigate of the line
    gloriously
rises from the deep as the ocean's foaming phoenix,
her deserted decks awash all flames extinguished!
We watch her fade through thickening
    fog.
How nothing stirs—not even a ghost on board!
Her hoisted canvas bent to yards restored,
proudly she streams abaft her White Ensign
—and over the graves of the shrieking drowned
    in the clouds,
she leans on the corpse of air in the coffin of the wind!

Once There Was Only One

Once there was only one
ferryman to choose from,
(Charon the lugubrious Greek),
to ship our souls across
the Styx. Now there are so many
competing—varying in vassalage
as the contributions expected.
They are better accoutered than Charon,
flummery-tongued and arrayed
like birds of paradise—some seeming
to dangle cut price passages
—discrediting one another in addition
in the thrust and parry of competition,
clasping the listening conscience
like a praying mantis.
The ancient Pharaohs were fairer,
weighing our virtues and sins together
upon divinely attested scales
that could balance our *ne plus ultra*
against our indigenous *culpa*
down to a grain of sand.
Whereupon (providing
our deeds both fine and foul
maintain at least an equipoise),
our souls become self-propelled.

The Army of the Dead

War is the weeping of mothers and widows—boots
marching on souls, an army tramping on conscience.
This is the hole in the soles of the truth, patriotic,
political and pathetic, of duty and the horror—victory,
the glory and the gore of going to war! An army
of ghosts, vanishing for ever—self-sacrifice
in the good faith and trust that the cause was just
--the senders the seated, the young the sent! Bloom
of youth cut down like a flower and now visited
planted in Arlington's sainted soil—sleeping
in beauty in a dwarf white forest of memories.
An army of the dead that gave up its all to a higher
bugle call. Can we really believe this is inevitably
and credibly, just part of the great American dream?

If Only

If only we could be judged at our best, not cursed for
    our worst.
If only we could tolerate heated words in haste and not
    mistake
for hate to berate. How mean we can seem by sunrise,
and at times too good to be true with stars in our eyes,
while stony to the lonely who tug at the strings of our
    hearts,
yet taking it hard when hung by our own petards.
If only offspring could forgive Love's dearth
of marriages made in Heaven, yet falling to earth.
If only we fishers of faults trawling our nets
cold see our own carp among the catch!
If only the wisdom of fools did not gush from the
    fountain
of youth and let slip through our grasp the love that was
    true.
If only we felt secure on our final flight
—and remains of ourselves on the carousel be not
    unclaimed!

The Glowworm's Honeymoon.

Side by side and heart by heart,
glowworm passing through the dark.
Concertina-like they slide
slowly through the eventide.
In their path, a leaf there lands,
and in tears they kiss, hold hands,
thus they make fortuitous omen
good excuse to kiss again.
In this world so full of woe
how bright it is to spark and glow
when so gloomy other folk we know.
Is there elation equal unto osculation?
Glowworm answer: "Dear me! No,
lest indeed it be to glow".
And to glowings there's no end,
when two wedded glowworm wend
ways in amorous duality
giving birth to a fine plurality!
Now oft upon a summer night,
more mature but still as pure
—like twin stars above the grass
they'll be kissing as before,
but wing to wing and flinting galore!

Oonala and the White Ants Sleeping

Oonala and the white ants sleeping.

On the Australian outback the airstrip tarmac
by fiery embrace of solstice dragon's breath,
was an infernal Turkish bath steaming to death
pygmy trees and rubbery shrubbery.
The stunted growth were the fallen angels
of heaven's overheated horticulture.
Among them was the indigenous ambivalent
miraculous cactus, with its pregnant virgin
leaf giving immaculate conception
in desert manger to colorful baby berries,
flowers, bushes floribunda, like holly
—reminiscent of jolly Christmas permanently in Hell!
—

But there were glorious inhabitable regions
on the eastern coast of the vast arid continent.
One had been specially chosen, long ago
by Captain Cook, close to today's lovely
city of Sydney. England having lost its American
oubliette to Washington and Marquis de Lafayette,
Cook was looking for a replacement forgettable
penitentiary for an overflow of convicts back in Britain
—as far away from trouble as possible. And Eureka!
he'd found it in a cove opposite the Barrier Reef.
—

What a contrast with the hinterland outback.
The latter was a vast flowering uninhabitable prickly
nothingness in nowhere, where pears grew upon thorns,

but an inherited Heaven for its aborigines to roam
and call their own—until one fateful December
the freed convicts took over. They had carte blanche
to do as they pleased with the defenseless aborigines.
The freed wretched underdogs became host
top dogs and shook off the poor primitives
from their backs like so many fleas! They did worse:
—

In Tasmania particularly cursed, it had been massacre
and its sepulcher, during that "Reign of Terror"
—taking of territory by terror, acquisition by extinction
—prosperity quickly by perfidy—and perfectly legitimately
at the time! Horrific tales of the holocaust
was handed down to every tribal tongue, father to son.
How could they have resisted blowpipes against guns?
—

Banished in their own beloved homeland, Chief
Oonala and his homely tribesmen would pray
to their pagan gods to coexist in the white
man's sacking of their ancient rightfully primeval
inherited habitat. But it had turned into
God's ungodly garden of untold misery.
—

The pale ex-jailed, after serving harsh sentence
under heat, rigor and the lash, were now released
as respectable citizens in a land without cities
or amenities. It was the promised unpromising
land to tame, steal from, fence in for themselves
wherever grass could be coaxed into growing
by means of seeding, drilling and sprinkling
from fortuitous copious artesian wells.

Anglo-Australian legalized citizen-less citizens
speedily urbanized and pasteurized the parched
wonder wasteland. Sheep were their salvation
—how could they fail? Who sweating under the
blazing sun wanted to wear wool? They could
capitalize and thrive thereby, exporting it all.
Thus very soon the devil's hospice
of British justice turned—startling as thunder
—into The Brazen New World Down-Under!
—

In quality and quantity of fleeces it could compete
with the Brave New World, the motherland and its
bleating wooly suckling child New Zealand.
The future was dyed in the wool. Industrialization
finalized the equation and the answer was the need (and
greed beneath) for oil. Expediently they could explore,
then drill for below the feet of the defeated, pushed back
into the outback, with the equally unwanted dingos
wallabies, rabbits and kangaroos. The outback except for
valuable artesian water, oil and minerals,
to the usurpers was not worth a kangaroo's hop.
Thus give back the useless to the unwanted!
—

Subsequently, the birth of jet-birds grew
into the jet-set, horseless horsepower,
lightless night life electrified by turbine
daylight, while the rising need (beneath the greed)
was for gushing gruel to feed transport as its fuel
—a national priority. And Oonala realized that the white
supremacy under duress were not to be trusted. Was
their new policy of protecting the aborigines as an

endangered species realistic—faced with the dilemma
of an airstrip violating the sacred burial ground of the
white ants sleeping—the hallowed
white cows of the superstitious aborigines?
The greatest sacrilege since the white man walked
on water had now been committed. Oonala
as chieftain and respected leader was outraged,
galvanized into action. He must consult his gods.
—

It was a classic case for astral council. He blew hard
on his digerydoo (native version of the Swiss
Alpine horn) and faintly and quaintly the spirits
answered in the rarefied air of spirit dialogue.
"Ye born faithful to the profound Formic Faith,
lie ye down immovably on the barbarians' tarmac
fouling with glutinous blasphemy. Do your duty
with impunity and they shall be given cause to repent
their infamy—and may your gods go with you.
The wallabies and the kangaroos, shall protect ye too,
and the virgin cactus with silent voice shall rejoice
with a beauteous flowering of her motherhood's leaf,
while the white ants shall slumber for ever in peace".
And Oonala did as he was bid, leading
his doting tribe boldly onto the runway,
where the desecrators were refreshing
with Foster's frothing home brew
—nakedness stripped and dripping to the umbilical
cord now tied to the hovering sword of Damocles!
—

But Oonala knew they were vulnerable in confronting
the questionable reformed beer imbibing angels,
proven to be like Fate—unpredictable.
For Faith as a defender is but a Job's comforter!
—

Shearer and sheep by kangaroo leap
produced prosperity's golden fleece
and everything was subjugated to its dipped
blowfly-free pure twenty-four soft
white gold carat purity.
The aborigines especially, if they got
in the way could expect foul play
—were like weeds in the garden of Eden,
uprooted would be if choking the seducing tree.
—

Particularly were they a prickly thorn in the side
of oil prospectors expecting them to vanish
at sight of the magic of mechanical might,
like the supermen arriving by featherless flight.
—

Oonala they found irremovable as a mule
galvanized by a straw for persuasion! Pink in the face
and red in the neck, the white man tried every incentive
in vain to regain the whip hand.
Dialogue was dismally unpersuasive
—cans cascaded to and fro to tickle toes,
but beer rewarded with but good cheer!
Mercifully, murder was no longer a solution
as rule of thumb to men with gun.
Legislation had swallowed insouciance
and regurgitated the makings of a conscience.

—

The spirits' displaced disciples
downtrodden Down-Under—how unfortunate
being where they were, as unwanted as the
wandering wallabies, the sheep-raiding dingos
and immigrant rabbits of fertile habit running
wild and multiplying from hole to hole,
and boundless bounding kangaroos
with peeping child or two popping through
mother's marsupial apron pocket.
They were all, a leap, a bark and a jump
out of time and place in that hot oven of
subsistence cooking in Hell's outback kitchen.

—

The white man's bird served as a vital
shuttle service fluttering between the evergreen
and the ever-arid scene. But a quicker
than hovering wingless flight had acquired
the required runway, but inauspiciously immobilized
by the defenders of the formic slumbers—stalemate!
This contentious yet comic sensational situation
was a lit fuse to a trial by fury!

—

Oonala was proving to be the prickly pear
thwarting all exigencies to be plucked from the tarmac.
The ants' burial ground had been defiled,
so lightning could strike, thunder sunder,
the earth in a fountain of ash could erupt
to bury the earth's crust as it must,
rendering both sacred and profane into dust!

—

In the heat, the seducing cans continually rolled
but with diminishing hope of achieving their goal
regarding the recumbent thinking in terms
of the cataclysmic consequences! Checkmated,
the men moved to their tents to alleviate
their woes in a liberal flow of Foster's placebo,
while Time crept like an aged snail.
—

As far as Oonala was concerned,
the trespassing wingless devil bird
of unknown mechanical origin
had come to disturb the white ants sleeping!
—

The oil men knew they were as hopelessly
outnumbered as a hornet in its swarm, apart
from the fact of the handicap of stings withdrawn.
—

The hours dragged measured by frustration
effervescing from Foster's froth imbibed.
The empties rolled as a tarmac surfing tide
to tickle the toes of the encircling foe
merrily giggling like children—to the last
innocent overgrown suckling child to the nipple
berries of rubbery shrubbery motherly Nature.
—

Three days went missing
and the squatters were still vociferously
but passively resisting.
It was victualed by meals on legs
for all transport was by the tireless
wheels of the soles of their feet,

the unbreakable food chain of providence in evidence
as the consummate consequence of Oomala's
    leadership.
—

The stalemate resulted from failure in all
attempts to checkmate, but fortuitously, the losers
were boozers, while Fosters beer could foster the illusion
that the elimination of frustration was by inebriation!
Time was itching to be lifted
as they put it on their waiting list
—no doubt until the beer ran out!
Meanwhile, the frustrated men would retire
to their tents to be inspired by their premier elixir.
Finally, the pink elephant ghosts passed
through their television's glass and en passant
showed the losers to be no heros in the pubic eye!
From the diabolical oracle of the headlines
and their media voice-overs:
"Macho oil men foiled
by deadly white ants sleeping!"
—

And understandably, the smirk on the spokesman's face
by the oil men viewed of the man reading the news
launched forgettable unprintable quartet epithets!
—

Wallabies hopped out of hiding chewing leaves
and occasionally a kangaroo or two to perceive,
glided by to eavesdrop on the proceedings
—the unnaturally dormant outdoor dormitory!
While animal sympathies were totally with the latter
and not with the quartet-letter supermen.

The pendulum had momentarily swung to a stop,
Dame Nature had played havoc with the clock
with a wallaby leap back on the dial of progress.
Time had run entirely out of petroleum,
the wilderness, over the wonderland had won.
All was now an oil drill to a standstill,
and its fountain "capped" by mishap
—inactivity crowned with perpetuity,
except for a rattled HQ!
In Sydney city calling frantically constantly,
armchair critics who had never ventured farther
than their own backyard, commanded action
from the outback to cap the deadlock! Grown men
indeed unable to deal with pushover childlike
primitives! What was the kangaroo world coming to
—believing in the satanic power of white ants sleeping?!
Was this not the stuff of fairytales and dreams?
—

But to men framed in their frustration it was akin
to a situation gaining less inspiration than inebriation!
Forced to capitulate, they were helpless and stunned
at the unforseen and uncontainable outcome.
To add to the mocked men's misery,
the aborigines in the cross-legged Yoga stance,
perchance provoked as they joked, enjoying
brunch à la carte on the tarmac and jollying
in typical apish grinning and grimacing fashion.
—

Chief Oomala rose, and gloating with satisfaction sat
like a squat messiah frog agog with his own sagacity
on a pond's brink, blinking blissfully to freckled kin

bubbles blowing across the dark water rippling.
Victory he smelled by the spell of the spirits,
as that frog well might at the foe put to flight.
At sight of the enemy leaving to clear entangling
growth, the tang in the air of tar was convincing sign
that the ants' star of ascendance was starting to shine
and at last that of the defilers on the decline.
For the hallowed burial ground had been abandoned.
A new black magic carpet was about to be laid
for the white man's birds of mysterious static wings
alighting in the outback by the good grace of the
    spirits!
Fascinating entertainment it all made
to astonish the prowling dingos,
hopping short tail rabbits the same,
and many a long tail marsupial to follow.
Oomala proudly addressing his tribe
in his native lingo timeless as moss,
exclaiming: "we scared the pale dingos off,
we brave protectors of the ants, wondrous wallabies
fabulous doe-faced kangaroos.
What a tale to tell our grandchildren
—the day we held the drilling dingos down
—without a fight we held the dingos down
—we did, we did! We men we did, we women
too, we did—we held the dingos down!
And with the help of the spirits, the ants,
the wallabies, kangaroos and digerydoos.
Together, we held the devils down, down, down!"

The Miller's Daughter

In the blow of a hill an old windmill,
the miller, a bachelor, and slave to his sails.
On weekdays he ground, on Sundays made hay,
while soon came a daughter oven fresh
as an April day in the shower of his doting eye,
her own the blue of the brightest cornflower.
And oh, she was fair beyond compare—her hair
like winded sheaves of wheat in the summer air.
But gossip whispered among the golden ears
—that suspicious unblessed birth a cuckoo's egg!
Nobody was April-fooled by the turning sails
and the miller making hay! Time has sped
—proud bachelor and laughing daughter in harness
are seen like sunshine happily grinding their harvest.

Never Too Late for Love's Lottery

When from its rosy apple, Time has peeled
the rind, and youth's flavor faded to the core
—yet freshness left for seductive lips to score.
When chips are down, ultra violet cosmetics
—how blinding to behold from fluttering eyes
gambling dangerously, like a moth dicing
with a flame. O the yeaning for the burning!
We Winter Garden gamblers our partners trumped
in our minds undressing, like peeling a peach of libido
—for ladies are delicious and more beautiful as lilies
unadorned—unequaled as sleeping beauties.
Love is fantasy's magic fairytale
we play with our lives. But never too late for a last
card—Jack of diamonds to Queen of Hearts.

None Wiser Than the Foolish Heart

Why pontificate to hide the self-evident?
The simplest foolish heart is wiser than the wiseacres
of the gospel haloed with religiosity. For Love
at very best is supreme innocence of compassion
unconditional—not contingent upon abject slavery
of worship. Whatever the pious doves of loftiest
flight may proclaim, together with all the saints.
A single tear shed for a poor suffering
creature more Heavenly than a whole kneeling
congregation. Believe me, there is a glut
of unnecessary kneeling, and a famine of genuine
feeling better placed—for instance, for what we
are doing to our beautiful planet we habitat, equally
with the animals. Are they *all* well and welcome?

The Soul's Laundromat

These machines take all coins of cares of the day
and generally the mind's dirty linen *per se*
The tongue's proprietary washing powders chug
with low sudsing to deal with run-of-the-mill
stains of the conscience, but powerful oral solvents
are added for stubborn giveaway lipstick on the collar.
Sorrows washed out, every semblance removed,
plus evidence suggestive of decadence hidden in
    bed-linen
—all fabric bleached pure by chloride of fabrication,
and spin-dried fairytale fresh.
Then home to the ironing board to press out the lies
—for stowing with little sachets of lavender to
    deodorize.
Thus Love is seldom the heart's undoctored product,
so forgive the cleansed and revitalized by the soul's
    Laundromat.

The Riddle of the Middle Sex

Take for illustrious example, Shakespeare or Da Vinci,
who but the Creator knows why neither were born to
sleep with a Juliet or a Mona Lisa? But if they were God's
creation, Nation or its president is outside of the
    equation
—and parrots in the pulpit should perch well clear of it.
No one knows the answer to the ageless enigma
Heaven-made. Thus *quod erat demonstrandum*
all true loving marriages are made in Heaven,
and no dragon for the valiant Camelot Knights of
    Chastity
to slay in quest of the sexual Holy Grail.
Hell and the devil were created solely by ourselves!
Compassion and tolerance are the whitest doves of
    divinity.
The riddle of the middle sex will not be solved by prayer,
but If good enough for God, why not *laissez faire*?

Holy Holocaust

Wars are the unspeakable
committed by the inexcusable.
What right is settled by might
without bloodshed by the misled?
The war to end all wars
ended ultimately in Hitler,
the Archangel of Evil!
Bombs for Peace
speak persuasion by annihilation.
If this be only half
the truth described
the rest be wholly half a lie!

When the Moonlight Breaks

When the milk-light breaks on the moon's dead eye,
and the slate night hewed from quarried cloud,
fainter are the stars than the homebound fishing fleet
ploughing the phosphorous furrows of luminous sea
to the gulls' whetted shriek—a razor of hunger.
In the gusting wind on the smelly-fish quay
the boy-man stares long in his turn
at the helm, while the dream is his and the boy was I.
—
Fishermen mending their nets and reeking of tar,
a girl among them caught my roving eye
and soon she became the siren of my wanderlust
—more love than lust, while I strove to earn her trust.
Now fled the days when love we made, and ebbed
the years or yearning for Love's old song.
The man-boy stares at his returning tide
with a shell to his mind and brine pearl in his eye.
—
I learned my raw craft to the sea made fast.
When the moon slept, the sun woke, and at noon,
was taught the sextant's part in fixing ship's position,
a trifle more positively than with Columbus' crude
    astrolabe!
In the full-steam of youth, I signed on a grubby
trawler tub that somehow to Archangel chugged
without sinking, or running-out of coal or souls!
I deemed it a miracle, but skipper took it in his stride.
—

At the grossly misnamed port of angels, we bunkered.
Our skipper imagined the less than White Sea
was an inexhaustible fish-silver mine unexplored.
He was mistaken. The wily cod had forsaken and North
we chased past Bear Island—almost to where
the bear fished through the hole made by the Pole!
Days were nights and nights days, in the beautiful
treacherous twilight, glacial continent so surreal.
—

Berg Dolomites followed as Death's white shadows.
Our pendulum of a vessel rolled itself silly and began
to land more sea than fish, freezing immediately
it struck the deck, heaping till our unstable old tub
threatened to turn turtle! But seasoned seamen
be survivors—not by life-raft, but by sea-craft!
So all hands to the shovel—breaking our backs to save
our necks—miraculously, without *wearing* the ice cap!
—

So went I on rusty old smoky tramps,
I came to love so well, and found I had exchanged
heavenly Hell for a hellish kind of a Heaven!
Having explored the killer Arctic—now fanatically
the homicidal Atlantic in convoy, dazzled by my gold
sleeve of command when on watch Olympian on the
    bridge!
but less vaingloriously, the war to end all voyages!
'Twas the last I saw of the big white paw.
—

Cod I chased nevermore, but ate on a plate
from the galley brought, while we ourselves were chased
and decimated by the moonlight's Nazi basking sharks,

on the Devil's Atlantic exterminating blockade. Every
 lunar
ray we spent contemplating our grave-sides
legs of wax burning—to melt into Paradise!
And whenever fog turned in the sun's milk churn,
in its whey, it was akin to collision disappearing into
 oblivion.
—

When bow is the plough, pulled through furrows by
 stallions
of wet canyons, and the wind is blowing its *own* whistle
witches are astride their switches shrill in our shrouds,
and the helmsman is hypnotized stunned by a
 thundering cloud.
In between moments becalmed flying-fish overflying
our deck, feed themselves to our frying pan!
How false is peace to we rabbit-scared trembling
and otherwise pretending as stalks the dangerous
 moonlight!
—

That Dracula of Danger, ever haunts the Atlantic
 graveyard
—vampire of the yellow-blood of the moon. Our
 smoking
funnels are our tombstones engraved with our epitaphs,
 read
by the merciless cunning conning towers of the Nazis
those voracious submerged shadows like sharks onto
 blood.
Never are we safe. The slightest trace is a giveaway
—a faint stray ray from our portholes black-eyed

and the Nazi sharks would sink their teeth in our
    topsides!
—

Our escort pedigree Shepherds sped in vain
possessing but milk-fangs for herding the lame
back into the fold. And for saving our coal-fired,
semi-retired, bottom-of-the-brine, overloaded,
embargo-beating freighters—their bones ever breaking.
In engine hospital, surgery constantly undergoing,
a score too many, essentially, for guarding efficiently,
our ranks of tired old tramps felt mightily insecure.
—

In the lunar limelight, our nerves are the whiskers of
    seals
feeling the predator approaching, yet nowhere to
    conceal.
Desperately, we cringe in our shivering skins clinging
to our thin masks of credibility, the crew convinced
we be given at least the milk-teeth of a lion
to deliver from the enemy by the gift of inspired
    leadership!
O awaken the mistaken! Beneath our shining gold braid
Apollo is badly shaken and not totally godlike!
—

When the moonlight breaks, it is the Midas touch to
    faded
braid seated on a powder keg, albeit less brave
than gold-plated! Yet its reassuring sunny sleeve
of command, the enlisted timid inspired. For the
    logical
survival of self-sacrifice is sea wisdom,

and the acquiring of its sagacity only by experience
—true seamanship salutes not the Admiralty
    Handbook!
However, forever, a little voice inside me whispered.
—

Whispered whenever the moon was a lover strolling
in its silver mist hand-in-hand with our hearts,
and asking: "Why are we at war when, but for the glib
of politicians, we'd be peaceful sheep of the deep, with
    a myriad precious sheepskins saved—not dipped in
    the Atlantic!"
How duty was the patriotic word that served to answer
all questions, and forbade any Doubting Thomas on
    our logs.
Could the pilot of our conscience be none other than
    God?
—

In and out the merciless moonbeams that so favored
the foe, we zigzagged to and fro in strict formation
—elusive crabs of elusion, for the foe was not fooled
—the enemy could wait indefinitely—he had nothing to
    lose,
sooner or later a straggler would drop out
and be fair game—a pot at a sitting duck!
Silence was the magic by which ships vanished
from sight to the enemy, according to hierarchy
    optimists!
—

Semaphore became the flagship of soundless
    communication
—royal navy flaunting to the peasant navy!

But critical were we of the Corvette-class pedigree
show-dogs, thought to be more showmanship than
    seamanship
—prone to endangering the prey along with the
    predator,
in their zeal for heroics—ofttimes, recklessly risking
turning us into wrecks by blasting friendly fire
—"charges" can be nutcrackers to foe and friend!
—

When the ocean yawns and sleeps ethereal beneath
her moonlight sheets, her lover is Death and never
at rest—his shoes are under our bunks, and we know
to whom they belong. And that soon we could be
    wearing
them like ghosts of Faith walking like Jesus on the waves.
The warning is written in the sky when the moonlight
    breaks
and oh, how we quake in our shoes of little Faith.
The lion within roars the courage of fear!
—

We recall how the moonlight caught fire to the Atlantic
in the titanic explosion that torpedoed a tanker that sank
with all hands at the drop of a sailor's cap.
Virtually every tanker is a floating coffin,
while every freighter in convoy flotsam afloat,
our lives expendable compared with our mission vital
to break the U-boat blockade. Every surfacing fin,
be it shark or dolphin could be mistaken for an enemy
    periscope!
—

Our worn-out-fleeces were doomed to the Atlantic dip

—and oh, what slaughter of our flock in one year alone
near half lost to the foxy U-boat sharks!
In that cataclysmic contingency Roosevelt appalled at
    the carnage,
sent timely assembly line Liberty Ships,
but notoriously prone to disappear without a trace
in heavy weather! And serving us sacrificial pickled
    lambs
to Neptune's sea-mint sauce! But the blockade they broke.
—

Thus credit should be given equally to Churchill and
    Roosevelt
for their united effort in saving the Brave Old World
from descending into legend as the Sunken Britannica of
    Atlantica,
and Europe crucified on the barbaric cross of dogma.
Official view was save the ships and pray for the crew!
And we went about our duties smoking a cigarette to
    forget
that we'd been turned into freighter food-carrying snails
with salt on our tails! But for our shells a nation in
    starvation.
—

Moonlight was the Delila of danger, she flirted with the
    enemy
hiding under her skirts, while disguised in beauty
seduced us off guard. The silver-fish waves
calmed our nerves with their somnolent regularity as
    Heaven's
grandfather clock in the hall of the wind at sea.
—peaceful as the god of war pretended sleep.

We could hear our thoughts breathing relief, at least
the length of a cigarette or the fireflies of a pipedream.
—

All sailors are lovers, all are human,
surely all respond to the ethereal? But the Nazi
zombie is an exceptional individual, hypnotized into
    brutality
he's the glacial, racial, cold fish of humanity
fanatically frozen to duty, incapable of feeling
and as a sailor a piranha! Exceptions but few like the
    fated
Captain Lansdorf whose flag-draped coffin
passed me in the street in neutral peaceful Montevideo.
—

In convoy a following fin is seldom a dolphin's.
All are suspect—in our minds at all times manufactured,
with eyes on top like the retractable horns of a slug!
Our own were as owls scouring the moonlight for mice.
Outclassed were our guardian angels, more show-dogs
than sheepdogs and too few for the flock in the sheep's
opinion—usually but two per convoy spared
for cargo creepers—stragglers like our Grado, expendable.
—

But to the predator but a single sheep compared with
    our flock
—and with full-steam ahead, hopefully quickly
    forgotten.
But oh, what a lonely liquid desert is the ocean,
when its camel train has passed. Neptune himself
couldn't find us—a speck of deck wallowing like a
    walrus

in surf—a specter vanishing through walls awash
of mountainous Atlantic thirsty for swallowing a vessel
in distress drifting helplessly to its necropolis Niagra.
—

Not handicapped by the passenger liner's towering top
hamper, and sans homing hum of our silenced prop',
we could instill, at least a mouse of courage into our
    trembling,
most-mixed get-what-we-can-conscript kind of wartime
    crew,
some of whom have crossed no more than the Thames,
and were about as seamanlike as an oarsman on a
    boating lake.
We were losing them to the sharks at a most alarming
    rate
for able-bodied seaman only by the able are made!
—

Broaching, was the truck of our anxiety, while calamity
    struck
in our minds constantly—and countered by praying for
    a miracle!
Captain Newton's inspired "Amazing Grace"
was engraved on every sailor's brain, and upon drowning
on his tongue, as a ship succumbed to a torpedo's
    thunder
and went under in the agony of shivered iron and lives,
while the lone-wolf-wind howled at the moon ogling
her beauty to the swirling water its obsequies
    whispering.
—

Our geriatric engine on its mechanical sick bed

undergoing terminal surgery, had breathed its last.
And the kiss of life as a pentultimate resort had failed
—our hopes for miraculous recovery cutting short.
The moon eclipsed into sunlight that caught no sight
of flag or funnel. Nothing but the rodeo of ocean
prevailed betwixt horizon and our drifting hulk,
desolate in the season of holly, mistletoe and good cheer.
—

We relied upon the Admiralty's mother of invention
    "degauzing,"
—said to reverse the polarity of homing torpedoes
—a miracle coinciding with our arrival at the bottom of
    the ocean!
We were between Scylla and Charybdis. Bereft of power
(the whirlpool), and the rock (our sitting ducks),
while our luck was walking on water. Our decrepit steam
    cockle's
corpse was unable to move a mechanical muscle,
even winch, for the anchor chain had been taken off life
    support.
—

With the unknown below and the storm brewing above,
on the Gulf Stream, we were bound for nowhere in
    particular.
Miraculously we drifted, evading burial in the
    overwhelming
avalanches of Atlantic Alps. Our distress SOS
changed to SSS (signifying a sinking by submarine),
ironically, in convoy was forbidden the air waves!
Omnipotent were the armchair Apollos of sea science,
while in awe we vanished as the haunting of lifeboat life.

—
The gale swept, ice crept, hail caned,
while drifted away the perilous nights and days,
gradually gaining longitude East—yet West
of potential salvation at sight of smoke or funnel.
At best we were the fleas of providence searching the
    hairless
for a host! Vessels could fetch up anywhere, above or
    below the ocean—prognostications by the "galley
    wireless's" crystal ball
—and a few of us at sight of a fin upon knees had fallen!
—

Then came rainbow weather, that reminded me of killer
    whales,
and mischievous dolphins—truant from schools of the
    sea
—and of a green-green glade in Glamorgan, where a
    siren
in mind was calling to her sailor hero across the ocean.
How Love is a spur that can convert a cur into a hound
—putting breath into pale ghosts who fear the most,
to exalt—be last in the dark to grope for the lifeboats!
O was she my very buoyancy keeping me afloat!
—

The night was ominously frowning over the ocean
threatening with its mighty mountains to plunge our bow
into serpents of phosphorous licking our waterline, their
    luminosity
danger transmogrifying into liquid beauty—till the
    weather
worsened, the mist thickening into milky fog,

while the air stood still as if saluting our fate.
Yet we brightened, aware that the more invisibly we showed
the safer out there where every ship was a target for a torpedo.

—

But our Fate was not as far away as my head in the clouds;
recalling the sweet laughter of a loved-one—so like
seeing her face in the glass of the moonlit water.
My beloved's smile in that mirror in my mind kept
my spirits flying for our faint chances of surviving.
"Hell! Hell!" I shouted silently to myself
as I realized that lives were at stake, while here was I
dreaming! And at sight of the fin I tugged the Turk of the bell.

—

This was the signal that galvanized all sea-legs
to leap from below and to swing out the lifeboat davits
—a sea-dog's chance for all hands to save their souls
from the holocaust unleashed that cut the cord of Damocles!
Even though the nightmare occurred so long ago
its horrors still rattles our bones till we wake in the night
—unstoppable as a raging storm or returning tide.
Heroes go under, but only a survivor was I.

—

O the gleam-green sea of war-tangled night,
its wild gray mares, its stallion white
stampeding twixt ship and iron shark,
that flings its one-minute foaming fin

to bury in our sundering thundering rust!
O the cries of the groaning blown sky-high
in a shower of bits and limbs—were as the shrieking
    flight
of gulls soaring from Hell, their feathers on fire!

A Hole in the Darkness

At the street corner they paused on her sightless walk,
her white cane like a crustacean feeling cautiously
the curb, where her guide dog waited anxiously
for a hole in the wall of traffic speeding unheeding,
the insensitive uncaring—the seeing blind to the blind.
Her precarious life expectancy meant absolute
    dependency
on her faithful adoring Labrador, her eyes in her
    darkness
of perpetual night unlit by moon or stars,
with little beyond love, trust and hope.
—

All alone, her chance of companionship other than the
    dog
seemed as slim as her cane. On the door to her heart
opportunity never did knock. Winter was bitter without
    sun,
yet, whenever she felt the Labrador—the darkness shone
—the lonely are less lonesome at the end of a leash,
the bond of unconditional love complete is unique.
—

The dog instinctively sniffed as if it could smell the speed
of approaching fuel expended, on a vehicle's breath
as it sped, not hesitating to spare a second of Time
more precious it would seem than human or animal life.
On they swept between green and red,
while an occasional tarmac toad the ruby jumped
—in the pendant slung from its highway neck overhead
—amber, ruby and emerald—the jewels of peril!

—
Restrained, the blind lady patiently waited
—It was one of those dangerous days when the worst
     on the road
seemed fanatically bent on reaching Hell first!
Crossings were by an act of Faith and the power of
     prayer!
On this occasion who was she unwittingly visiting
—always at the back of her mind that Life was a gamble
—more so with her kind trusting entirely to her guide?
—

At the perilous ruby, the pendant of extinction,
the dog waited-waited—and the blind for the tug
to tell that all was well—the legal luminance
this time had turned to the priceless emerald of
     security.
—

The dog sniffed, while the old woman listened
with an intuitive cold sweat of apprehension, as she felt
the tug and heard through her agony the screech of
     brakes
accompanied by Hell's foul smell of burning rubber!
Then fell a darkness even greater than blindness itself.

Echoes

Time is gathering moss. Our village grown
to a town, familiar faces—the majority gone
to the churchyard willow letting her hair down,
the minister ministering to the angels, the craftsman
sold out to a hardware chain—Dame Nature
a prostitute selling her beautiful body to the plutocrats,
a swarm of industrial locusts, alighting on the countryside.
The skyway the Dawn Chorus of the jumbo-jets,
and highway the rapid throughway to the graveyard.
Leisure little pleasure as the yoke of Atlas,
role-model for success. Are we living-ghosts?
Love was once the steaming kettle of youth
boiling on the hob awaiting tea for two.
Sadly, out of the moth-holes of our dreams we flew.

The Last Waltz

In the park, deserted-dark—two seated figures
haunt the rippling lake. Night sleepwalking
on the moonlit liquid, reflects old Eleaze
like a beautiful flower gone to seed—the tight
thin petals of her unseeing eyes are closed for ever.
Otto, her devoted Labrador, is harnessed to her darkness.
—

Long before the dog became the compass
to her white cane, that other Otto and Eleaze
on that same park seat had sat as one
—bread from hands feeding somnambulist swans,
Nature's nesting angels on that gnomic water.
And in its ghost-glass the courting couple viewed
their own bemused sweet-selves kissing.
—

In that phantom mirror the wan moon waxes
—Past and Present coalesce in veils of virginity
with ballroom gaslight lisping to the strolling Danube
—freshness of its breath through open window blows
softly onto shoulders bare—graceful as gazelles
—coinciding with a breeze Eleaze now feels on her cheek
as the trees begin to bow to the swans at her feet.
—

From its inception, their love had been the doomed duet
in a haunted glass—reflecting the ghosts of gossip.
That other Otto and Eleaze in the gaslight hissing
—at an intimate moment when mischievous eyes were
　　looking
the fated couple had been caught covertly embracing.

—

O jealous forgettable wallflowers sighing bouquets
of perfumed unrequited yearning. How young Eleaze,
glorious among had been in whispering silk!
but destined to be zephyrs behind their quivering fans,
obliviously and innocently danced *la fille fatale*.
Bright as her tiara's sapphires was the sky of her eyes
at dawn before dusk turned them to pearly clouds.

—

She feels the Labrador's paw in wintered hand,
its veins exposed like the roots of the linden tree
where, a fathom below, Otto sleeps permanently,
buttercups and daisies brightening his shaded grave.

—

At her seat by the moon-beamed lake, it is as if silence
had fallen asleep. In Death's shadow she sits
savoring memories uprooted from the linden. Otto
licks her blueberry lips that from cherries had turned
—that the Labrador's namesake had picked when lips
    met lips
that spurned. And wasp of waist had stung straying
hands—teasingly before they came to terms
—the tender surrender of the genders to its opening
    fruit!
It was long-long ago, when the peach out of reach
was finally plucked and tasted to the stone—innocently
so swan-like, she recalls, by Otto alone
—when Love was its gadfly loving and gadding to its Fall.

—

A breeze autumnal leaves again exhale
  —Eleaze inhales crisp memories—the countless

suitors dismissed, the handsome, the rich, the persistent.
Otto leaps to lick her lips, while his ears she fondles
and feels that other Otto at her fingertips.
She doesn't wipe off the kiss—in her heart it is *his*
who sleeps beneath the linden. The dog bristles,
sensing a presence—sensitive velvet twitches.
Eleaze drops her cane. Mystic strings
begin to sing, a maestro ghost of bygone
ballroom fame materializes—the years retrace
to bustles laced and graced with butterflies of ribbons
—gliding to the gorgeous galaxy of lovely legs
that lilt to waltz and hands to partners changing.
—

She feels his white glove—a settling moth
of cotton cloth on the slender lily of her moist
debutante's skin of her virginity touched tenderly.
—

And now in the park the moon at last is melting
into the sweet melon of mind-watering memories.
Trees in their shirt-sleeves, swept are shivering,
but Eleaze feels warm in her love beneath
the gaslight stars—she is electrified by the sudden fact
that Otto is staring into the pearls of her sightless
    cataracts.
—

Pale hands the darkness clasp—her flute
of a voice, flits blueberry lips, as blindly
she gazes into burnt umber canine luminance:
"Otto, dearest, on my *carnet de Bal* I've reserved
for you the last waltz." And as if to assist Eleaze
to her feet, Otto lifts a gallant paw.

—
The strange couple linked, foot to claw,
hand to paw, burnt umber to pearl
facing each other, bridging the tacit void,
the *doppelgangers,* of Past and Present coalesce.
Adoring Labrador with clawing encircling paw
on mistress's arthritic hip, wags and barks
at the blanched face crinkled like unlaundered linen
—as she dreams—ironing the wrinkles of lost love
laid to rest in the shade of the nostalgic linden.
—
The gas-lit stars are so silent in their nocturnal
    chandeliers
that the fallen leaves could be heard sighing in their
    dreams
as strolling invisible feet began to whisper.
An owl hoots gray wisdom to swans rippling,
stirring reminiscences of largesse spread from hands
of a long-dead romance by the same lake—the same
haunted mirror in which they'd seen themselves kissing.
O how it all into mind came back like a boomerang
flung by the mendicant swans and the oracular owl.
—
From Space that oracle hots at Eleaze and *Otto*
partnered in their dance macabre. Dangling tongue
panting dewdrops drooling—the duo slide,
widely glide, bow and slowly pirouette
—as waltzing in their prime possessed long-long ago
in a ballroom—and haunting with phantom ears
she hears gaslight hissing from the starlight chandeliers.

Poetry

One day, bards of a bright New Age
Renaissance will awaken to give the crows of Parnassus
a singing lesson, for but larks relate to Heaven's gate.
Croaking invokes no thrilling resonance to haunt
the captive heart and ear. Let spring sing
of the ins and outs of family matters—nests,
berries, necessities, yearnings, yearly catastrophes,
like the bare boughs of winter creating hunger.
Coventry Patmore—of irregular pentameter professed
of no importance how many syllables a verse possessed
as long as only five in the reading are stressed.
The spontaneity of birds cannot be surpassed by the
    Muse,
the cardinal of words—but let them be touched by such
as a mouse in mourning for its spouse in the claws of an
    owl.

Going Global

Do we need to fade in a hundred degrees in the shade?
Think of the poor hot Polar bear
in shock, sweating in an Arctic Turkish bath!
How unpleasant for fish boiling to death in the ocean
of global warming. Think of the formal over-dressed
penguins trading white tie and tails
for bikinis, Nature's negligee! Think of the breathless
panting crocodiles on the shore grinning no more,
and birds of the air blown everywhere by the hurricanes
—the same for reindeers without cause to jingle to St.
    Nicholas
with lost power to his sleigh, plus children without toys
on Christmas Day. And so fatal for the planet and
    inhabitants.
As an overheated owl hooted: "the humans behaving
like animals, and the wild animals like humans in
    disguise!"

Great Call of the Sea

O give me a ship, the wind on my neck, a deck
at my feet, tall masts to scratch a sapphire sky
and what cradle of peace rocks to the maternal deep!
Her canyons in liquid beauty cleft, her foaming
    mountains
with snowy crests to a vastness luminously green,
Neptune's natural monuments more monumental than
    manmade
crumbling in acid rain—and pastures more ethereal
than sheep may safely graze. With hand to the helm
what beautiful albatross spreads her cotton wings
—O how she flies like a hawk from the glove of our
    dreams!
To life as a shadow, a sailor is sunshine, akin to the
    childlike
dolphins playing with their toys of the ocean, and their
    giant
sonic cousins, spouting their fountains so supreme.
The wind only knows whither we blow, for she's a lover
like no other, and larger than Love. What treasure to
    measure
in the pleasure of leisure—such a joy to cast off
from the wharf of life and rejoice to the tongue of the
    tide
under shrieking clouds kissing the shingle goodbye.
For at sea, what comradery, at the table taboo
politics and religion, for more sins are brewed in the pot
of these heavenly twins than by their virtues rise to
    Paradise.

How we sailors long for the innocence of our kindred
 spirits,
like those gray friars; the gulls—a far cry
from the cries of the city, the greed, the grime and the
 crime!

The Captain's Spirit

The wind blows him to her heart—her mariner from
    below
the sea. His ship had struck a reef in the teeth
of a typhoon. Now she hears the rattle of death
and a fluttering of wings in the haunting coffin of the
    wind,
as lightning sears the telephone wires with its scythe
of fire, sweeping thunder loud—and she listens
to that lost soul shrieking in a sea of clouds.
—

Once she faintly believed in the old salt's
tale that drowned seamen rise from the waves
to haunt the churchyard graves, but suddenly she truly
believes in the gospel of gulls. For she sees one sitting
on a commemorative marble tomb containing no bones
—only a name as its revered remains. The gull
is, as his parrot repeats, the captain's spirit!
—

The nautical bird wears an able-bodied
seaman's cap, doll size, and worn
at a rakish angle, as if doomed about to capsize
—just as its master had and frequently required
to adjust, as the bird did now, with its claw, as she saw
so remindful of her spouse—the lost love of her life.
—

Able-bodied seaman Polly and the captain had sailed
together, bird perched on his master's shoulder
in fair and foul weather, from sleepy doldrums
to Neptune's raging rolling mills swinging

the crow's nest crossing the raven of sky
and kissing the crests of snowy avalanching mountains,
swamping the hatches at every dip of the scuppers
in the foaming ocean's beauteous lathering suds.
—

There is brine in the tide of the sea-widow's eyes
ebbing to the sunken horizon of a glorious sunset
romance. She hears his feathered shipmate speak
like the ventriloquist of master's voice, from its cage's
    perch.
In her mind's nostalgic telescope she sights the disaster
and in horror watches the schooner as she sinks surreally
out of mind in a vortex of swirling foam
—as the parrot repeats: "Seaman Polly reporting
rocks ahead! Seaman Polly reporting
rocks dead ahead, dead ahead!"
—

And the engulfing swishing wash swallows her
    heartbeats
and her lungs in an icy cave of ineffable silence!
A moment later, she is electrified as the clouds break
forth in their tumultuous timber-cracking unrolling
linoleum of sound, while lightning's spurs prick
the flanks of stampeding trees in the dark forest
of stormy night. Under the violent rocking
of the cage, its door flies open and the bird
is soon perched on the widow's shoulder! Skin
and feather flee together to the window facing
the cemetery, where the gull is sitting madly screeching
on the mariner's empty tomb—freezing the widow's
flesh to the marrow—as the bird with the predictable

fateful words repeats—shaking from beak to tuft, wild as the weather hammering the window: "Seaman Polly reporting—the captain's spirit! The captain's spirit! Rocks ahead! Dead ahead!"

Endless Horizons

O blow me home to the whales, the beautiful fountains
of the ocean! Let me inhale the ozone, the noggins of
    Neptune,
to toast my escape from the noisome rat cage
of trade. Only Love is the miracle to hold a candle
to the moon of tides. My soul is aching for our urchins
the dolphins, our happy clowns of the water circus.
From your towns be rumors around to say you must
all sweat, yet not be equated to your crooked crust
in your dull dog-eat-dog barking kennels,
where the Alpha chews the meat and the pack the bones!
Not so with us roving sea-hounds—we're for everyone.
O blow me from your polluted blowholes—to the
    rolling sea
that cries over our shoulders to whoever craves to be
at liberty, as the wind that freshens the faces of the free!

Trees

Shedding her beautiful tears, how glorious a tree!
When her hair turns to gold, she weeps and our feet
begin to whisper in sympathy. O High Priestess
of Loveliness, bless us with your sheltering green sleeves.
What ambrosial umbrella to our showers of eyes. What
    relief
we get from listening to your choir practice donning
your blossom surplices for evensong. We hear in the
    wind
the hymns of choral societies to which other birds
belong in the vestries of the leaves. Cardinals of Autumn
and bright Bishop Robbins of Spring join in
the general rejoicing, adding their lyrical voices
to the psalms that greet our ears. And oh, how poignant
to perceive the mendicant friar sparrows receiving
alms from the poor boxes of their parish feeders!

Nature's Traveling Gentlemen

Sweated by the sun and kissed by the moon,
two ragged gentlemen of unrestricted leisure,
Nature's tramping tortoises of the tarmac
were slowly nibbling up the mileage,
by their shark mouthed boot leather.
How they were being passed and over passed
and bypassed by road rodents of the
passing pleasure, as fast as shooting stars.
And among them few Samaritans
—noted more for velocity than charity.
Nor could the devil have driven faster
and with less caring for life and limb
in his flaming chariot of fire
—on his way late for a date in Hell!
—

And it was fireball weather
for shark-mouthed boot leather
to be traveling on the highway
en route to savor
the shrinking countryside,
that robs the animals
of a paw in paradise
of their own usurped heritage.
Likewise, to the poor pilgrims on foot
to the Mecca of Nature-worshipers,
were losing their precarious oasis
of diminishing pastoral beauty.
—

They did not have to be told

that heaping wealth is fool's gold.
Time alone is treasure—time to sit
a lake beside and watch a dragonfly go by,
or nothing at all if so inclined?
But who can complain
we gain nothing from their lives,
yet prosperity is always at a price.
In the Gomorrah of the Dollar
they made no contribution
to consumer distribution
or taxable fossil fuel pollution,
while on their way by shoe leather.
Nature's traveling gentlemen,
harm nobody, their conscience
is rag's moral sanctuary,
while what harm do they do anybody
including busybodies so alarmed?
They brave our speeding dangerously
surviving by a miracle,
light as Jesus walking on water.

Beyond Comparison

Could Love be the tender imposture, the ultimate
    splendor
that the sky of her azure eyes may engender, when
    peeping
between passing of weeping clouds? Could it be
    snowdrops
posing as forget-me-nots pinned to her fair bosom's
    exposure?
Could it be a juniper strolling like lavender hand
in hand down Honeysuckle Lane?
Or multiple choices among homely voices
hoping to dangle like diamonds from devoted lobes?
But never science for not capable of romantic reasoning.
Perhaps an Art form, as it is profoundly in the dark
like inspiration waiting to be ignited by a spark?
Could it be a swan plus rabbit of habit in part?
Or a beautiful flower propagated by divine seed
blown in the wind and falling on a fertile heart?

No Second Spring (the toxic truth)

Gone are our bleating lamb days
leaping wild our innocence
(by blame) still unstained.
Yet Youth, how it was wasted
on Youth, till in truth, no wiser
turned our fleeces gray.
Now, after long years lived
in little fear of fleeting
into passing sheep,
we mourn above everything
no chance of a second Spring
in Life to sound the Alpine horn,
recalling our lost lambs to the mountain.
O those joyful foolish yesterdays,
where laughter rang above the fray.
Where have they gone
where have they strayed?
Gamboled over the hill
and far away!
How lush the yellowing
grass was once
before the echoing silence!
In vain we blow
to our mountain hollow,
but now only our memories echo.

A Day to be Free

We hasten, you and I and our little dog
(with maybe a small child or two)—then let us both
thank whatever powers may be to have escaped
for a whole precious day from the treadmill of trade
grinding out the National needs synchronized to greed.
We welcome the respite to breathe the blessed rare
    release
as we flee on our fleet rubber wheels to the sea
—our island kaleidoscope where wishes flick dreams,
Crusoe sights a sail homeward bound
—from the yacht club! And Man-child Friday
chases a turtle in the shape of a crab on the sand!
What would life be without make-believe?
—

O to douse our tired toes in the tide,
while our flea of a terrier jumps around sniffing
crustaceans and other imagined perilous predators.
Our children wander to exciting adventures in their
    promised
land of sand—with buried treasure to hand.
We watch the drunken crabs staggering home
from their rocky taverns with iodine on their breath.
    We lie
lazily under Heaven's ultra violet
lamp in our free solar tanning parlor.
Meanwhile, brine is pickling Time and our toes
bathing in the swishing sudsing swirling foam.
Soon, a salt breeze on our skin is blowing
glowing pink as we up to go roving.

—
We tread the sea grapes, in the sand flies' tarantelle
—those clumps of champagne vines that pop so well
to the pressure alone of the uncorked soles of our feet.
A scout gull cries and the entire troop
swoops from a cloud to share our picnic feast.
One steals sardines from beneath the layers of lettuce
leaves, tomato and cheese. Gulls are equipped
for making a phenomenal exit from their thieving crimes.
—
Our whirlwind of a terrier returns to orbit its tail,
while our children practice their powerful magic in
    emptying
the ocean with their pails. Distantly castles built
once accomplished, demolished with remarkable skill.
—
Leisure is frying in the hot pan of Apollo,
a sugary radio Romeo is crooning his solo
till becoming unstuck by rapid flick of the switch!
Sudden minstrelsy from a telephone tick interrupts
stinging and adhering to a nearby sleepy ear.
Then once more all is quiet on the water front
and surreal to the comatose around as the "angels of
    Mons."
Even our fox terrier has gone to ground
with knight flies seeking the grail of its tail!
Neptune triumphant with trident spears a shark
basking in the shallows like a man-eating shadow
contemplating a tasty two-legged snack a-la-carte!
Paradise regained, our turn to confront the knight
flies of the seaweed of Camelot—boldly we challenge

to a tournament, with broadsword of aerosol and lance
    of parasol!
—

Battle cries having died and wind out of breath,
paddling little legs have sped
while their bowlegged diaper-padded croissants have
    dipped
in the surf. Shrimp-faces in newsprint spurt
sound like timber being sawn! Ears
kneel to coffins of fishes haunting the wind.
We slaves of our disturbing urban high-rise
propensity for intensity, sip the eternal primeval
mystic solace and savor the lift of spindrift.
Thereafter, all is somnolence, smiles and laughter
—as a dolphin dreaming and seeming so fishily human,
mirroring a mermaid (with his flippy whale's tail)
cooing to her horses with white manes of the main.
Evening squeezes her glorious orange in a cool
glass of breeze, and our heart's thirst is slaked.
—

An ice-cream ghost materializes, ringing
his wedding bells, summoning screaming marriages
to cones dripping confetti on the crustacean
    congregation.
Diminutive vandal hands litter the sand
with paper cups and gooey plastic spoons.
Aunt Bessie blesses bride and groom
off to lollipop honeymoon, while terrier with drooling
flycatcher tongue is coveting a sticky licking.
A winged wayfarer of solitude, a sandpiper, is digging
for its dinner at the water's edge washing its legs.

—
The wind blow-dries the sand at the ebb,
vast to the horizon becomes the shore's stretch,
and dormant land has gained the upper hand.
Reluctantly at last we must pack our things to rejoin
our bustling void of toil and noise. Our glacial
marriage maker, divorced by a cone—returns
home to his own sticky offspring waiting.
—
Nostalgia overwhelms. We recall our naked nascence
of innocence, counting in our highchairs with slide rule
beads of baby mathematics-cum-rosary
of the nursery. The rolling shingle jingles reminiscence
as tiny feet toddle to their parent's vigilance.
—
The moon has wound her tidal grandfather clock
and swung grandchild from brine to a mother's side.
Our meandering flea of a terrier meanwhile, is a barking
typhoon in pursuit of its cyclonic tail, plus desert
crossing caravans of crabs, the nomads of the sand.
—
Left alone on the rolling dunes, we drones
of the workaday swarm, look on, drooling from our
    minds
recalling clones of ourselves when lollipop-young,
loud in our cries, soaring to Paradise by mounting
momentum of our playground's pendulums pushed
by doting elders—higher and higher and louder
nearer and nearer, till almost within earshot of an angel!
—
O for the baleen of a whale of a wind engulfing us,

and the sea swallowing its diurnal burning fireball
smoldering into glory as the soul's Aurora Borealis!
Heavenly to return again and again to revisit
our ephemeral lost childhood's fairyland, akin
to those vacated coffins whispering fish obituaries
—our phantom listening shells of haunting memories,
sweet clams whence all our dreams began!
What would life be without our days to be free?

Fateful Attraction!

To the penguin sex is taken coolly, as a kind
of glacial Arctic after dinner mint.
The horny snail is slow, yet quick to mate,
the snake has a long history of slimming for love.
The tiger in Niger is gloriously glamorous to a tigress
in striped pyjamas making amorous overtures.
Hairy as coconuts is the big baboon
by moonlight, and likewise the spunky monkey.
Bare bears make beautiful brides,
sweet as honey to their great furry grooms.
Happy hippos are gigantically passionate, rolling
in the mud, bonny and sunny and peaceful as doves.
The Polar bear has a lovely white wedding.
In the twilight faintly we hear: "Come sweetheart
All is not lost—dearest defrost and try again!"

The Beef and Pasta of Art

Concrete pasta, the marvelous mortar mix
by Rome invented by phallic Manhattan inherited
rising to the plumes of pollution—a bird's eye
view of high rise bureaucratic enterprise,
bridging eyesore for the commuting labor force,
to its omnifarious urban best endeavors perforce.
Romans had viaducts for it, Greeks a word for it,
and the Brave New World a spaghetti junction
of highway unction of genuflecting knees of
    throughway!
—

In perfidious Nero's dynasty, the transport macaroni
created the incredible overhead flowing viaducts
while under head and under seat flowed
the Tiber to the elite seated like battery hens
on marble multiple-holed toilet plinths,
 male and female elbow to elbow while below
them flowed the viaducts in conduits conducting
    effluence
to estuary, accompanied by loudest lutes discreetly
to deaden the deafening defecating crescendo! It was the
    Handel's
Water Music of Ancient Rome and bridged the primitive
jungle drumstick to the thumping conductor's stick
beating time to Beethoven's ear trumpet, up to the
    modern
baton of Aaron Copeland and Benjamin Britain.

And It bridged the Tiber and the historic Seven Hills

of ablution to pre-Latinate culture,
when Aristotle and Socrates sat upon a stone cultivating
the grass roots of wisdom with the figs and olives.
—

The visual arts is currently a bridge between
the classic glorification of the beauteous female buttocks
by Botticelli and the Dutch connoisseurs of erotic
    nakedness,
(natural as a bumblebee extruding from the nectar of a
    flower)
—and the novo-Titan-Titian modern abstraction
in all its baffling buffoonery of avant-garde to amuse
and bemuse the haunting gallery culture ghosts
vanishing from Matisse to Pissaro to materialize through
the radar antennae of the finely tuned mustachios
of Salvador Dali as a disembodied spirit—as a self
—proclaimed kin of surreal paranormal inspiration!
While Art has dissolved into volcanic introspective
    eruptions,
perspective exploding into lava of color and presented
to the public like the head of John the Baptist on a
    charger.
What baggage the eye deceives and the mind appeases!
And waffles of color trickling like treacle to tempt as the
    gourmet
appetizers of meretricious modernist initiate adulation,
masquerading as Art' appointed gifted connoisseurs,
while never ran color but in avalanches and rushing
    rivers
depositing their overflowing silt and sewage onto
    canvas!

—
But it's ersatz art, because no childbirth of an evolving
    wunderkind.
it's simply resurrection of ancient bones from China
and Japan—immortalized by silk worms chewing into
paper made from rice in place of rags—representing
a kind of Kimono delicate Geisha School of etching in
    relief,
as opposed to the cruder borrowed facsimile—the pasta
    and beef!
—
Behold the budding balding Pablo Picasso,
matador tycoon of "Oxo" cube art,
and crafty craft, visualizing prosperity in controversy.
So to Hades with chiaroscuro—and paint noses flat,
faces like flapjacks with a bit of this and that
so nobody knows what the genius is driving at,
but bound to be "discovered" as the new bone to lick
by some name-making critic—a trick of the trade!
And Pablo profited by spontaneous combustion
    daubing
a fortune tossed onto easel with the ease and panache
of a chef with dough from his hot frying pan!
—
Thus the corkscrew nose semi-comatose
dead pan pizza movement sprang
from the loins of the new lucrative enlightenment
at the speed of light, esoteric avant garde
in all regards. Pablo soon added Leonardo's
versatility to his pallet knife, including extra-
marital wives to his anomalous modeling collection!

He diversified brushwork by ironwork and ceramics—
    chipping
and sizzling with the Olympic torch of oxygen acetylene
with expertise unsurpassed by the robots—welded
    Japanese
automobiles. Incredibly profitable, it invited comparison
with Van Gogh, a greater talent yet selling but a single
canvas in his entire tragic life span
—ironically to become the richest corpse in history
—an unlit blaze of delayed spontaneous combustion.
—

The movement went into a trance branching into
    transcendental
soporific Surrealism, that from its somnambulism never
    awakened,
with Salvador Dali as its dormouse Dali Lama,
put affectionately into the Alice-in-Wonderland teapot!
—

The avant garde adopted a strange enigma—Rousseau
middle-aged, short and self taught
—naive, trick-sleeved to gain applause.
He painted the African jungle on safari to the Paris
Zoo and its botanical gardens. His tigers were elongated
almost to snakes, with sinister resemblance to faces
of detractors! His monkeys had grimaces equally
    reminiscent!
And why none of them appeared to have not cottoned
    on is a wonder!
All the long animals prowled in a luminous
ferocious zoological tropical botanical jungle.
a maze of intertwining twiggy centipedes of leaves

caressing the canvas from ear to ear. Patriotic
Republican Rousseau never deserted his native
boulevards of France, yet he left a tropic legacy
that can vie with Gauguin's Miss café-au-lait Tahiti!
—

Into flatter perspective still, prostrates the printed page
as raucous crow preening unabashed and unadorned
—the rough Hessian of current eclectic verse
has crossed the ponderous bridge of no return
in a stately carriage without wheels to spark
the cobblestones of our hearts and weary souls.
And somewhere between Chaucer in trendy doubloons
and cavalier with lace and laughing face
lutes to his lady over his patron's shoulders,
while Love's fair blossom is seasonal as its song.
Great paintings in words take ages
to dry—meanwhile, are prone to be smeared.

Delicate Vision!

I have phantom ears that can hear butterflies stealing
from the buttercups, daisies supping from the sun.
And the petals of her eyes mascara putting upon.
A myriad miles away, me she has forsaken
—yet in her soap suds, I can hear the bubbles squeaking.
I can feel fireflies like starlight walking on air
as once was our love so fair. Altogether, my vision
is a wonder—though as the tunnel of a mole,
blindness of a bat, I have night sight. And from my
    pillow
I can see her faintly like a fairy at the bottom of my soul.
When the sky is lit by its beautiful chandeliers
a pair of fruit flies forever appears
nibbling at the luscious slice of a melon of moon
—as we ourselves, once upon a dream had seemed.

To an Anonymous Lover

As fond memories stroll like lovers on their paths,
I think of you as my desire's dazzling solitaire.
Your secret lover am I, and you the treasure
buried in my heart. I am the painter of your beauty
while your goddess-nakedness shines divinely to inspire,
as I paint in the darkness your portrait in the air. And
    there
upon ephemeral canvas, momentarily I view that
    portrayal
and declare so beautiful that even Juno arrayed
in all etherealness is envious in paling beside the
    sapphires
of your fair eyes and the willows of your pendulous
    hair!
In the wondrous world of ocean, where whales spout
to Heaven their sonic prayers, and dolphins ride
the rainbows of their leaps—I a sailor, hear
a hornpipe to your portrait, and before it I am kneeling.

Sparrows of Paradise

When the lark is carrying song
as a bouquet to an angel,
and heaven the mother of blossom,
even the trees are lovers.
But lowly human sparrows are we
ours are not nests of swans.

Occasionally we foul our nests
seeking fruit sweeter than the rest,
the elixir of love made from pears
only to discover
Chinese peaches sweet and sour.
We lack the power to eat as angels.
So we travel through storms
and hail of the heart
in quest of the god's divine pablum.
—
Looking up to the stars for guidance,
we open our Pandora's boxes,
and preen our best bed feathers
ready to meet gods and goddesses.
We see Venus so bright
by heavenly light
we fall in love at first sight.
And alas, at last maybe,
like the moon melting
into Arctic twilight
 more lemon than melon!
—

When we click like crickets
in their hidden holes in space,
humming for ever,
we can imagine ourselves
part of that throbbing mystery.
 Ecstatically we fly
from clover to hive
to be kissed or stung by its queen,
or a bumblebee,
as the case may be.
And we levitate!
For those who follow
in the shadow of moonlight,
sleep in the valley of darkness
to wake in the luminance of love.
Ethereal be the lust on our lips
that meet in silence behind closed eyes.
It's like the throbbing essence of the coalesce
in the courtship of bees with the flowers.
Poignantly in the presence of a crescent
moon promising beginnings renewed,
we open Pandora's box again.
This time shall we click?
We hear the haunting harps
of cicadas scratching their backs.
Though love be green as the leaves
are brown we do not lack
fidelity of the imagination
and fragile promises
invoking sweet pollen!
—

The star of the great white bear,
puts its paw on our chart.
Cerberus, the twinkling Dog
in the kennel of the sky,
is barking at Venus
at the end of the leash,
while to gods and goddess
of loveliness we waft in a surreal
world of harmony orbiting reality
at the speed of dreams,
becoming emotionally airborne
and as miraculous on cumulus
as Jesus on water!
For we are walking on a cloud
— sparrows of paradise
crickets of the black holes in our souls.

The Drifter

How green was the gangling, liveried elevator-
    grasshopper,
green-eyed, green as naive in his uniform.
And descended from his suspended cage in the
    workplace,
tweedy-reedy as a skeleton, bristly as heather
no socks in shoes, elbows patched with leather
—socks holed. This is the way they saw him,
the well-heeled looking down at the down-at-heel.
Like passing ships in the night sailing without lights,
the invisible indivisible passing the superior
    supercilious
—numerical code communication by digital automation
to succinct command of single spoken syllables.
He was the quintessential living green ghost,
vanishing through a wall of indifference on Fridays,
    materializing
at night, but for Saturdays and Sundays when he drifted
    from sight
into his secret universe—as a nonentity in the land of
    plenty.
—
Passively he elevated the hierarchy to their bureaucratic
    heights
—seeing their anonymous scarecrow disappearing below
free as a breeze on his off-button breaks
—his mysterious black holes in unaccountable space
in Time uncommitted to conforming to the ways of the
    lave.

The money spiders envied the drifter escaping
from their web—while penurious leisure envies lucre.
Time had a clock and it ticked off the bellhop
at dawn by card in his slot in but payroll recognition.
Now released, and whistling the favorite tune of his
    beloved
Jack, the flea of a dog on the bite of a bark,
the drifter dropped out of Time like a gull from a cloud.
—

But short-lived was the ecstasy. Back he had to be
in his green hair-shirt nightshirt for the night shift
of their phallic office tower, sheathed in its condom
of stiff concrete, flourishing the National flag,
symbolizing the stars of architecture in striped pajamas!
—

The uniformed ghost of vanishing hours elevated
the lofty giraffe bureaucrats to the top of the tree
and the humbler moles to its roots, while the homeward
    bound
scurried to Exodus, below where the devil in denims
shoveled coal in summer himself to boil,
and in winter lightly to toast his superior sinners,
sinning in comfort and style. Meanwhile, the grasshopper
clicked and hopped non-stop to the control
of trellis prison gates of the plush penitentiary
of plenty, with busy worker and shy shirker
precariously poised on the payroll on permanent parole.
—

The bellhop was the spectral fly in the supervisor's cornea,
the ghostly mote vanishing through the smear on her
    spectacles,

as she powdered her suspicious nose in the powder
    chamber
of the impregnable fortress of confabulation, the ladies'
    room,
where lipstick tacitly reported to mascara with
    devastating
fire power, aiming at the aimless and defenseless
grasshopper for the tongue's petty target practice!
—

He was as anonymous and unassertive as a Moslem in
    purdah
—his importance minuscule. Who but negatively spared
    him a thought
other than the kindly cashier at the cafeteria, counting
three doughnuts occasionally as two, and not charging
for the sandwich, as he hesitated and fiddled, holding
    up the queue?
And maybe the girl with sunshine in her blue eyes,
flitty as a butterfly as she talked altogether about the
    weather?
Not forgetting, his dog, trading barks with a walrus
through his master's window facing the Bronx Zoo.
The privileged animal (like the landlady domiciled on
    the equator
of respectability) had illusions of grandeur, having
    humans as servants
in constant attendance, plus its private swimming pool!
—

Anabel's mother was as grand as the walrus, with live-in
    Hispanic, and
another for shaving the lawn, trimming its sideburns

and whiskers of the hedges, plus red-pimpled bushes
of horticultural puberty.
—

The landlady's daughter was mother's sacred cow
while an "untouchable" was her lowly lodger—
    forbidden to walk
on the same side of the swimming pool as Anabel,
but the maternally-approved stocky stockbroker was
    made welcome.
When the grasshopper as an insect passed her toasting
    her beauty
in bikini distantly at the water's edge, he felt
tiny and futile as a firefly flashing to a star.
Yet she remained in his daydreams, the bone of
    contention
buried in his underdog's panting heart, howling
to the moon—reminiscent of Jack mistaking himself for
    a wolf!
—

Perpetually being fired, and leaping from job to job
as continuously as running water, what hope had he of
    proposing
to a girl like Anabel? Suspended by a cable
between Good and Evil in the Kingdom of God Almighty
of Creatures Great (commercially) and Small expendably?
For peerless ruled His Majesty from his penthouse throne
of heaven, with his wingless Archangel elegantly soaring
to worship on the highest pair of heels in Paradise,
and taking the secular sacraments with a holy
    peppermint!
In the lower echelon were the angels of executive flight

and the laptop pharoahs embalmed with aftershave
for the after-office-life with the angels groomed
to follow thereto demure in haute couture.
But the grasshopper was in outer space, not in the Limbo
    of Libido,
so related to no heavenly body in his galaxy of fantasy
to worship but Anabel orbiting her swimming pool.
It was a lonely suspension dangling on the monotonous
    string
of sporadic bell-ringing and gate-clicking
in the numbers lottery of the million-to-one chance.
—

And the scarecrow therefrom forever longing to disappear
—not to scare, but feed, the hungry crows and be
    pasturized
by the unequaled peace and beauty of the countryside
—the idle pursuing the idyllic as a way of life.
Anonymously and unmissed, he vanished into his secret
    universe,
uncursed by industry—the solution to evolution by
    pollution!
The "untouchable" needed to remain in touch with the
    corners
untouched by the heavy hand of industrial Man.
And in a meadow somewhere, shady lush and cool
beneath a tree, lazily to lie upon the grass
  glowing so reminiscent of Anabel's swimming pool.
With his little dog in arms, he would find his way
free hereunto with Jack barking gratitude
to every good Samaritan of fortuitous travel.
—

Time, that catcher of toil by the tail, with the grasshopper
failed to prevail. He was a green ghost vanishing
into non-ambition. With no calendar to conform to life
is simplified, the future a mirage, the present all that
 matters.
When life is a dream, it is always Autumn and in Winter
still bearing fruit, though tasted only by the feet
whispering memories—the crisp leaves of the heart.
—

Unfortunately, a fool's paradise haunted by clowns
juggling with the bubbles of destiny and more than
 occasionally
one is dropped, be it only a trifle, but gathering
momentum in the magnitude of rumor, snowballing
 into globular
proportions, as each contributor embroiders. That
 figment
of the negative imagination we call fate is never
too late to cause mischief. It could bring even a
 grasshopper lower
to earth—with the help of his own harmless tongue
that had dared to impugn the sanctity of the salami
 under the glass
dome of the president's sandwiches—and duly reported.
Don Quixote de la Mancha of munching had tilted
at the very windmills of heaven, that fed every head
from the devil shoveling coal to the exalted above all.
—

The sinner had likened pork on fork to an act
of cannibalism! He could squeamishly imagine the
 salami squealing.

It amounted to heresy among the carnivores of the
    cafeteria
Mecca of the worship of gossip. It dunk speculation
into the coffee of conversation, false as the flowers
    eternal
in vases, ersatz as the marble tops of the tables.
—

Back to his rocket with doughnut in pocket, oblivious,
the drifter would drift, while indifferently his absence
    was missed.
How could he be dropped a hint that anything was
    amiss?
If an executive spared more than syllables it would be a
    miracle.
—

Slipping happily away to the countryside,
he would suck pastoral serenity through straw in mouth.
He took adoring Jack along—as naturally right
for each other as cup and saucer belong.
There were inexhaustible creatures to bark at and a few
    to chase
till the cows mooed home to milking time
blissfully unaware how their poor country cousins
were naively grazing their way to the gravy chain!
—

On one memorable occasion a passing billionaire
    financier
sped them to his fabulous farm by his lightning-strike
mechanical goddess Mercedes, that terrified terrier
and grasshopper alike! Badly shaken, the drifter
descended to regain lost rapture in pastures

peaceful on their Samaritan's green acres of agriculture
—sun under a glorious blood-orange counterpane.
—

Free to wander at will by lea, meadow
and rill, it was bucolic bliss just to be part
of all this—to feast on moonlight serving peace
on a silver tray of its rays to the daisies and cowslips,
spiced with a whiff of new mown hay
—while halcyon to lie in the dew-moist meadow
ear to earth with its small life throbbing
round Mother Nature's sheltering apron strings.
And to leap the style—be beguiled by beauty undefiled.
—

Whistling to Jack in arms, they sauntered to a brook
tickling trout, while in a cloud a lark forsook
earth to sing in heaven, and giving the crows
a singing lesson. Jack joined in with a bark
to deafen every threatened creature in sight.
And a sprightly grasshopper in Nature's own uniform
jumped into the drifter's lap, without recognizing the fact
that one grasshopper had just introduced itself to
     another!
—

After a fly-buzzed catnap under a ballet of gnats
on their delicate points performing silently on air
somewhere near Jack's sensitive ear
—it twitched in alarm and he woke with a loud bark.
And to a light chorus of circling gauze tutu,
the grasshopper soundly dreaming also came to.
—

It was time to move on closer to the garrulous brook

faintly heard still whispering to the sleeping fish.
Soon thereafter, Jack was flat on his back
in dog dreams interlocked, and time forgot
by the drifter dangling weary feet in the crystal
waterfall. And oh, so cool in blissful pensive
repose feeling the lisping gentle cascade
trickling sleepily through his tingling toes!
—

Time gathered a modicum of moss, and inevitably
it came to pass, as all good experiences
are doomed to fade—the night shift beckoned.
Two thumb-rides later, Jack was barking
at the walrus and the drifter was clocking his crust's card
—refreshed and ready to rocket by his numerical
    buttons.
—

In his tea break, disaster exploded in his face

from the money spider of the payroll (not the slight
    trace
of sympathy), as she handing him his pay packet,
with dismissal note to chew with the now flavorless
    doughnut,
for the news had frozen the last bite in his mouth.
—

If only he could bound with Anabel, that lovely gazelle,
to the boundless sea! But even in the event of such
    miracle,
that miserable brown envelope would not suffice to pay
for even one day at a romantic seaside hotel.
—

With that cheerless prospect in mind, he took tray
to trash—his last to the clash of kitchen cymbals
and drifted into the street. The city was a Christmas tree
of fairy-lights—a magic necklace of stars
hung from the neck of the Hudson's suspension bridges
—as far as the eye could see to the nostalgic domain
of Anabel, overlooking the water of the talkative walrus
bragging about its own private swimming pool
to Jack, barking back through the open window.
—

Almost sleepwalking, he drifted to his lofty lodgings
and entered like a corpse tiptoeing in a morgue. Not a soul
was around and the silence of tenants was profound—a snoring
hog, but for occasional voice filtering cracks
in slightly tainted territories—marked by cats!
But the little dog had finished its conversation with the walrus
now hobbling through dreams on the crutches of its twin tusks.
—

He passed to the death rattle of the archaic elevator
serving all floors to the seventh where the lark sang
at Anabel's heaven's gate, and lonely Jack
barked at her treats dropped through the letter box.
No uniform graced this decrepit sparking conveyance
elevating its humble tenant worker bees
to their respective leased quarters in their people-hive
with its landlady-queen's ears a listening-sting.
His heart missed a beat as he skipped out of hearing.

Anabel in heart and her mother horribly in mind,
he made the hazardous crossing to the archaic elevator.
—

To clicking of iron he entered to the familiar
    pyrotechnics
gasps and jerks of the last legs of motion
—a far cry from the workplace's mirrored version
—a luxurious perfumed closet of pendulous perfection.
By comparison the landlady's was the death rattle of
    motion,
a tired tortoise levitating under psychic hypnosis
—and hesitant electrification by press-button persuasion
aided by prayer and curses at pressing in vain!
Suddenly, he felt the clattering cage accelerating,
but it suffered a massive stroke midway between floors!
Between third and fourth it gasped its final breath
choking to death, groaning on its scaffold cable.
—

Had he not the experience and agility of a sprightly
    young bellhop
trapped he would have been—but he managed to spring
    free
to exit in a matter of seconds, launched into darkness,
for light bulbs thereupon had given up the ghost.
Pandemonium broke, doors opened, mouths
opened, cats meowed, dogs barked,
people barked, shouted, swore aloud,
while the grasshopper hopped anonymously under
    lucky cover
black as a bat hanging from the claws of their cloaks,
as onward, upward and heavenward, step by step

he crept, panting breath by breath until, exhausted,
euphorically astonished at the miracle, finally he fell
into the arms of Anabel. Simultaneously (as if psychic),
  Jack
scratching frantically at the door, unseen behind,
sensed all was well and not worth an extra bark!
—

"Don't speak, mother's listening!" She whispered
like a mouse feeling a cat at the tip of its whiskers!
Longing and joy then mingled with smudges of lipstick,
while no courting birds rubbing beaks could eclipse
that ineffable spontaneous erogenous limpet of a kiss!
Later, in bed, pillowed on her ambrosial breast,
with Jack at their feet like a swan in its nest, the
  grasshopper
realized he had leaped from a high-rise to Paradise!
And the bellhop had hopped out of space and back in
  the race
ahead of the stocky stockbroker in leaps and bounds
to unlock the secret chamber of an angel's heart,
with Anabel's golden stolen keys of heaven!

Autumn Twilight

O lovely ladies, your beauty is like an everlasting flower!
How mascara has brushed new luster
on the fading petals of your violet-shaded eyes,
above rubbed old-fashioned delicious-smelling roses
above the velvety carmine tulips of your still luscious lips.
As we walk our feet begin to turn the leaves
of crisp memories, the laughter mingled with the tears.
As a painter can enhance Dame Nature, so beauty
survives maturity by gilding the lily, albeit it is
the flower that dies in the shower. No matter—naked
and unadorned more adorable to the bewitched. As
    roses wilt
before their plastic kin, the beauty of a woman is
    externally
as eternal as her loving soul within. Her tinctured
    autumn
can turn the lustiest lustrous leaves of youth.

Box Car Barney

Box Car Barney, bard of the greeting
cards, sold by the railroad locomotive verse
clicking to the track's predictable signals, smooth
as iron wheels rolling to their whistle-stops.
His shop was a cardboard box, the necklace of
    commerce,
and the hanging Babylon of charity with hand dangling
a cup—the cash register of the homeless. Nothing
clicked in his life but coins dropped to the Muse's
mart of saccharine Art—pretty as cardinals
on a feeder—tweeting to conscience—sowing seeds
of hope sprouting silver bell honey bee
congratulatory oratory, Christmas reindeer tinkles
and tinsel, birthday wishful sugary sprinkles
and lovers' trinkets kissed by hearts and flowers.

Sea Peace

Tall be the masts of our bygone seaman's craft
—not a screwing iron duckling quacking the pond,
but a silent wooden beautiful billowing swan
of peace with cotton wings and ribs of oak
—caulked with oakum redolent as a tropic breeze
—tight as a clam for all that can be thrown by the
    ocean.
—

And I'll take the helm, as a seasoned seaman able,
making fast straining shrouds to the masts
—with sheets to hand to thrill to that leaping porpoise
of a plunging bow ploughing luminous phosphorous
fields that yield the harvest of herring gulls
dropping loud from a cloud. Nowhere as fresh
as the bracing ozone in the moon's magnetic tide,
with stingray on skin and crab in my rolling stride.
—

Between the tidal flow ashore, evermore
was it so, since swains spliced roving hearts,
and wished upon a star that love be plain sailing
—but when lips link lips, not a pail of wisdom
between them! For Love's leaky Leviathan is seldom
a tight ship. Alas! a shrieking gull
at times! And at others drifting dispassionately in the
    doldrums.
With soaring euphoria our precarious romances embark,
love-levitated, we flounder, blinded unwise
by its sun in our eyes as we tread the Sound's grapes
in Neptune's vineyards of the shore. Holding hands,

we watch the crustaceans rolling home from their
    taverns.
Our laughter turns so easily to tears—gentle on the
tiller to steer clear. In vain on the storm
we are worn out pouring oil on troubled water.
—

When the tongue lashes like a Westerly gone mad,
let us cast off the wharf of bitter wasted words
—dump our duffle bags of worldly cares
on deck and log-on to a faithful peaceful swan!
Ever is the anchor we drop in harbors unsafe
to drag in the fouling mud of regrettable talk
bent to mistaken thoughts. The mind is a maelstrom.
Ironically, much mischief is stirred in its witch's caldron.
Love never was the spliced heart's tight ship,
in salting eyes we inflict our stinging spindrift
—yet fond memories leave behind their fated footprints.

Portrait of a Kiss

In my orchard
of fond remembrances
hers was the freshness
of an apple just picked.
In her studio apartment before
our youth had gone to seed,
upon her bed spread
our limbs,
while above our heads
the sacred
open heart of Jesus
dramatically portrayed
—a hint of chastity,
neither of us possessed,
for we were with love obsessed
and did all that hands could caress,
and with lips no less.
Her beauty is for ever
pictured tinctured
in the haunted glass of memory
—introspection, the exquisite
vintage liquefaction of a kiss
—an erogenous coalescence
lost since to luckier lips,
to become the specter
of the rose. Who knows
if we had our time again
would we see Jesus on the wall
like our own crown of thorns?

That first kiss of lips and hips
—would it be the Second Coming?
Or just the faded portrait of a kiss?

The Miracle

Her breast caressed by a crucifix, her Faith proclaimed
—an old widow, gray as her cat by night,
was nursing in vain her subjugate lover, a flower
in its window box. It was a sick plant, swallowing
sunlight with insatiable thirst, as its only appetite.
A rosary worn, like the Venerable Bede, her waist
encircled. She knew not her quiet inanimate patient's
surname, or if prefixed by some floral Latinate name.
The unknown species was a gift from her visiting priest,
who had baptized it at birth with heavenly holy water
from the font of the kitchen sink. But name or no name
given, an exotic plant smells as sweet.
Under the auspices of a Reverend Father of her Faith,
it seemed God had bestowed relief from her grief.
Though only a flower, it had been pink in the living petal,
but suddenly it was pale as her white cat settling
into her lap, as she sat at her window box vigil,
hopefully, praying fervently for a sign of recovery.
But the tortoise of Time crawled by, and it never came.
Meanwhile, the ghost of memories constantly
    materialized
and vanished in the void of her beloved spouse's grave.
—

He was only forty-seven—did God in Heaven
all-merciful need to drag him away so soon?
Could He not have waited until their wedding
    anniversary?
Why deny her the coveted photographs for their
    memorial album,

that mirror into the dawning twilight of happiness
    reflecting
morning, when Love made evening the rosary of sunset?
She knew her Lord performed in mysterious ways,
like the Trinity, and His sacrificial son perambulating on
    water,
but why was one of His mysteries the death of her plant
grown into her husband's image, as he born in God's?
Inscrutable as the bread of the body and the wine of
    blood,
was the powerful pill from the pestle of the Apostle's
    apothecary
absolving the Faithful from cannibalism when
    swallowed at the altar!
—

The flower was sick, stricken with jaundice of the leaf,
and sagging gradually to its knees, as if joining her in
    prayer.
It sank lower, as if trying to lay itself down
in its wooden coffin of the widow's window box,
ready to be buried in its own compost earth.
As for the widow, never was mourning greater than hers.
Unconsolable, rivers of grief ran down her cheeks,
  while they turned pale as the white cat in her lap.
The ghost of memory haunted and she saw her husband
in place of the plant. He was lying on the sofa—
    blueberries
staining his lips the color of a heart attack.
—

In her mind was a nostalgic echo, for the nectar of the
    dying

plant increased in its last hours—overwhelmingly
smelling so reminiscent of her beloved's favorite
    fragrance
—a bottle of which had always been his repentance
    distilled
munificently, from his janitor's slim pay packet,
whenever their marriage slipped from its Heavenly
    status.
To ensure complete forgiveness, he would also present
silk stockings for the cat to purr against,
and claw ladders in the replacements all over again!
Now, the stockings were holed as she shuffled around
in the whispers of slippers, uncaring how the mirror
    reflected.

—

Perhaps God had plans to resuscitate the flower,
in a manner naturalistic as the fable of the monkey's
    paw,
that once wished upon, the wish came true
—in a way that nobody knew from a commonplace
    coincidence.
This was the way miracles were perceived, she believed.
In a parable, she recalled that God chided the idle
—helped only who helped themselves, so it depended
partly on herself—and all would be well? Brightening
at a thought (monkey's paw in mind)—obviously
Heaven had placed in her head, she consulted a florist,
who sold her a cure for sick flowers. The miraculous
medication was duly administered in soluble form
to the soaked soil and compost in the window box.

—

Lit by the fluorescence of remarkable expectation, she
 waited
patiently for minuscule sign of a splendiferous recovery.
Not a leaf changed color, nor petal its pallor.
The Dark Angel was felt hovering overhead.
In the end it descended, and the beloved plant was dead
—under the hypnotic stare of the translucent pearls
of the sad vigil of the widow's thick cataracts
—cascading from a Niagara falling from melting mascara.
—

Any hope of plant revival was now up to God.
But where was He in her desperate hour of need?
Why was He not heeding? Had even her heavenly angel
guardian gone on strike—too many accumulated
calls on her extraterrestrial answering machine?
Heaven offering around-the-globe, around-the-
clock service for prayers, she feared God
could not promptly answer every earthly call
from weeping willows drowning in their rivers of tears.
The exchange in her mind replied, "All lines engaged."
God was busy. The all-forgiving was to be forgiven.
—

Dutifully, the due self-help (her rosary),
was whispered to—in "Hail Mary full of grace
the Lord is with thee," etcetera, as piously taught
by the convent nuns in the grasshopper-green of her
 youth.
—

In the local park the night was a raven.
No lover was strolling, no dog barking at Cerberus.
God had made everything propitious for a religious

magpie of flowers! Devout eyes looked about
cautiously, and saw a live facsimile of the dead
species in her bag lady's bag. Direct and swift
as the flight of a crow, the live and dead flowers
changed places, while not even the gardener could tell
that the latter had not died a natural death in his park
—after spreading a few fallen leaves to hide
the soil disturbed! God, her accomplice, was free
to break his own commandments! Her conscience was
    clear!
Yet for double indemnity, she lit candles to the Madonna
smiling like the Mona Lisa, as the coins dropped
in the box. The substitute sibling was undetectable from
    that given her
by the priest, so her deep secret was safely guarded.
The gardener in the park would scratch his head and
    replant!
—

"Who brought you that new plant," inquired her neighbor
when visiting, "you dark horse, you didn't tell me you'd
    found
somebody special—do I know him? Is he here in the
    building?"
"Of course you know him. He's in the building, he's
    everywhere.
Don't stare at me like that, his name is Jesus.
I prayed so hard, and eventually He resurrected my dead
flower like Lazarus, according to the gospel in the Bible!"
The cleaning lady had the wind taken out of her apron.
She adjusted her hair pins, as she stroked between
the nebulous roots of her Faith's hair line.

"Gladys, I wish I had your conviction. But like our priest
says, you can't beat the power of prayer,
although I must confess it does a lot less
for me, than apparently for you. Looking at that plant
—my gosh! Jesus must have performed a miracle!"

Prudence Primm

Prudence was a prim collegiate blue-stocking,
a spinster devoted to her catechism—akin to a church
    mouse
nibbling at Christianity. As candles on the altar flicker,
occasionally did her Faith. She took cat-comfort
in her lap. Tom was stuffed to the tips of his whiskers
with tuna, and spoonfuls of cream to fortify his milk
till purr inflated into fur. She was the most consummate
unconsummated lady of her locality, with Heaven's price
heavy on virginity—closing the gap to opportunities!
Sadly, she prayed for a suitor of purity to replace
Tom who'd gone missing without leaving a trace.
Months lugubriously lapsed, then Thomas returned
with his bride, plus kittens—rekindling her Faith.
    Prudence
in her pew sank to her knees, staring above
eyes like saucers—at her priest as if seeing God.

The Sadness of Green

How sad is green, when the wild wind blows
to the cracking sound of a tree uprooted by its bleeding
toes, a tree that in its green sleeves was dressed
in its Sunday best, cut by the tailor of seasonal
leaves, and throughout our lives a blessing on our jaded
eyes! What other mirage can there possibly be
the like of sunlight snowing on a cherry tree?
When in Fall her confreres let down their golden hair,
what shedding of glory can compare? How sad is green
that fell before the gold could tell what it was whispering
from its soul, before it fell from Heaven and breathed
its last at our listening feet? Once tall it stood,
an umbrella in the rain, and in the sun a glorious shade
while a monument more beautiful no man has ever
     made.
A redwood has stood the test of Time and higher
soared than sacred thoughts and inspired dreams.
Greater dignity and beauty no man has achieved
—loftier than any living thing touching both Heaven
and Earth, while loud in the wind is its song in praise
to a passing cloud, as thunder rolls by
and it remains unharmed. Did God intervene—or chance?
If the former; how could a tree be less deserving than
     another?
My mood is melancholy—how sad is the unspared tree
—weeping pain to the roots of its ruptured veins!

The Spanish Crabs' Tarantelle

Seaweed grows the grapes of Neptune
in sunny vineyards of the tide,
where all crustaceans of kith and kin
kiss by whiskers thick and thin
while others shake pincers of goodwill.

Sun and brine ripen the popping grapes
for the shapely shelly senorita's tarantelle.
They mull the wine for mollusks and crustaceans
—a crabby senor, mean of mien
is staggering home from where he's been
mixing his drinks—ozone with iodine
—while on a rock his lonely spouse senora
is patiently preening in her water mirror.

A pale faced cuttle greets with "Hi!"
lobster honey, have you been hiding?"
And tipsily he answers breezily:
"In the tide, sweetheart—did you miss me?"

The multi-filaments of vines
are lifted by the snakes of brine
to foam and hiss in rubbery rafts.
Soon belly up crabs are on the wind
like minuscule coffins tidal surfing
—their live-in corpses upward kicking.
A slim little shrimp with whispering legs
tiptoes to meet a handsome prawn to spawn
on Midwife Nature's delivery bed.

In vineyards of rocky lakes of grapes
the pretty senorita crabs
—the belles of shells in ponchos red,
raise their emerald skirts and begin to tread.

Sad Ladies of the Shells

Sad ladies of the shells, my dears, the dolphin
am I in the whispering echoes held to your ears,
as your tears drip from the petals of fair eyes.
Only your soul can see me, by the light of a star.
Take an umbrella to shield me from the rain of tears,
while Love stitches a rip in the weeping clouds,
their pearls of Heaven seeping into your beautiful
    minds.
O for wings of a swing—to feel your weightlessness
as with laughing eyes to gull-like cries—you fling
your soaring feet in featherless flight to Paradise!
Ladies of the shells, sip your tea-leaves in the sky
—the astrological golden tea, the ambrosia of euphoria,
the heart's dead flowers ever brewing nostalgia
—as you hold on to the skirts of an Indian summer!

Tinkles to Drizzle

Dimes from tight fingers drizzle into cups
—droplets of compassion that amount to not very much
thinly on the bread of the homeless butter to spread,
or, alternatively beer to bait the breath!
And why should we deny them that trivial pleasure,
for each in his own desert finds buried treasure.
For no hopers possibly pangs need a prick of the needle,
yet who are we to say that every dime donated
should be devoted to sowing for our haloed saints?
Thirst and hunger have no morality, who
should judge if thirst we slake and hunger
suffer? No hopers are losers not choosers
of the unfortunate condition they find themselves in,
while Samaritans dismount to subsidize, not
    breathalyze!

Coffin in the Wind

Sleepwalks the Past
of loving ghosts
from the sea shell coffins
in the burial ground
of the ebb tide wind.

There on the ebb
sadly I wait
on the burning sand
for your dead kisses,
felt as salt on my lips
from the spindrift wind
off the incoming tide.

Our toes in the tide
in the bygone of goodbyes,
your bosom was my pillow
and its soft beat
the drum of our dreams
—the stars their wand
when the sun was gone.

Empty as a shell
abandoned on the shingle
that night, our final
thoughts were laid to rest
with their last rites
to be whispered by the ghost
of a fish from its coffin in the wind.

Brother Rubberneck

It was six o'clock before sunrise
had speared the dormitory beds.
We woke to a clap of hands
and brief to-be-answered prayer;
but farthest from our minds
was the pious thought intoned,
as we battled with towels for basins,
and braced ourselves to face
the lying lips of the faucets,
the hot being as frozen!
While Brother like the shadow of God,
followed us everywhere.
—

Brother was always standing
guarding the holy-washed,
his teeth intermittently gold,
as he smiled white as the lamb of the Lord,
his expression between continuously lead.
His neck was curiously limp
and long like the turkey hooked
behind the pantry door,
which inspired us to give him his name.
—

They served us fine on Feast Days.
with oranges and blessings
and chapel and apple and prayer.
Centurion Brother of morals
leading his noisy legion
through sinful streets of town.

Then back through private churchyard,
to be swollen with jam and bread
and cesspools of boarding school tea.
Brother was raised on a dais,
like a guardian angel on a cloud,
gobbling and chatting to Brother,
sustained by special food from God.
Upon their table a bell tolled
to our sinful decibels.

—

Our Chapel voices melted
as prayers solidified,
into hymns of pious praise.
When the priest's serving chosen
snuffed out the altar candles,
corridors rustled with cassocks
overrun by stampeding sheep.
The atmosphere was crucified
by portraits of Christ on wall.
We crossed ourselves and mumbled
in our places for prayers and graces,
in the refectory to keep spiritually
body and soul faintly together,
while a rod of Divinity
ruled our uncertainty
as discipline bambooed
to stoical stifled tears.
The bleating flock pressed by
their fleeces shorn by conscience.
Nakedness dipped in Faith.

—

Days were punctuated
nights were terminated
by bells—sleigh bells in Masses,
cacophonous bells for classes
and to Vespers Sunday nightingales.
We woke by clap and slept
by prayer and lived between,
till the ringer was rung at last.
I remember the chilly knell
for poor old "Rubberneck."
Most solemn was his Requiem.
Our candled crocodile carried
his simple wooden coffin
to canting mouth of earth,
where it listened to prayer as we glistened
—and a few were not crocodile tears.
—

In class he had always stood
like an inviolable ikon on a pedestal,
his flock of knowledge overshadowing,
while somehow learning crept
between the cracks,
like a small mouse squeaking,
as the rickety stairs we climbed
slowly to teaching's heavenly heights
—chewing toffee to lubricate the brain
and take some of the inculcating strain!
Cassocks were Learning's lurking shadows
rustling through our lives
like a holy black forest
of greenest little leaves petrified.

The Pale Side of a Shadow

At one time or another, we're the pale side of a shadow
shared in the looking glass—the face sans trace
of Time having passed. Somewhat older
to strangers we seem than to ourselves and others the mirage
proclaiming to please—the mask of make-believe
we wear when the real beneath questionably compares!
But what is life without the tinder kindled?
O face of buried beauty just waiting for discovery
by a kiss from a lover in a pink mirror! Deceptive
but effective as a heart reflector. Who lives who loves
not blindly—the eye piercing the impenetrable darkness,
the divine spark igniting the dullest life?
Why not, since Love is the fantasy on the dark side
of the sun, and we awake from the pale side of that
    shadow.

Through a Glass Staircase

All about her we thought very strange.
No crow trod the corners
of her beautiful old eyes,
blue as sapphires by sunlight,
their corneas clear as dew
in the dawn of their smile.
—

A few dotards recalled her from their youth,
riding side-saddle round her estate,
followed by a giant hound
—before the ancestral mansion
was burned to the ground.
She was the arsonist herself,
some wicked tongues put around.
—

Now she lived alone
in a doll's house by comparison
with one servant for companion.
They came and went,
intolerant of their mystic mistress.
Each had a story to tell
—a few with profanities
concerning her sanity.
Only her Great Dane remained
ever faithful—not one,
but several at intervals,
for the giant breed were
naturally short-lived
—but a decade on average.

Thus nobody visiting knew
which among them was threatening
aggressively guarding his mistress,
as each was named Damon.
The Damon who addressed me
and caressed me when I visited
could have been his predecessor.
—

We few who came regularly
regarded her more sympathetically,
 thought of her as the dreamer
on the tall "glass" staircase
—because she said with a straight face
how, whenever she climbed
she could see through
to the cupboard beneath,
where there lived a hungry
little mouse that needed feeding.
She could hear it squeaking,
and it was definitely not,
as we incredulously suggested,
"a board creaking!"
—

furthermore, she informed,
as if it were the norm:
"Every old house has a mouse
and nobody feeds it"
—

She was said to be "out with the fairies!"
But we who visited her
knew her as one of those rarities

of all-seeing, all-feeling,
human beings,
half mystic, half psychic,
not insane but on a higher plain
where animals, humans and angels
were somehow anomalously the same
and did not fear to tread in step.
—

One day we came to visit
as was our regular habit,
to share her remarkable
experiences, insight
and fascinating conversation,
and exceptional viewing
of every conceivable situation.
—

But she was there to welcome
with her warm hospitality
that rivaled her many charities,
responding to just about every cause
—child that needed saving,
dog, cat and wolf craving
shelter and affection,
and of course, whale and tiger
distantly dying of hunger,
or afflicted with disease,
or by pollution or malnutrition.
—

Her last servant told us
that after obeying her mistress'
final instructions to place

best Cheddar cheese
for the little mouse
in the cupboard
—in its Delf porcelain dish,
she was struck dumb
by the terrible tragedy.
—

She heard to her horror,
her mistress tumbling
to her death! Rushing to the
hallway she found her lying
sprawled at the foot of the staircase,
but with no visible signs of injury
—no bruises, no blood!
—

"She lay there like a sleeping beauty,
her lovely clear blue eyes were closed.
She looked perfectly peaceful as if
she had died natural. It was uncanny.
And her Great Dane kept licking her face
as if trying to lick her back to life.
And when they took her away
in the ambulance, it howled all day
and night. The following morning
we found the dog dead on her bed.
—

"And do you know, sir,"
continued the woman,
 "that board don't creak no more,
no matter how many times we climb
that ghostly staircase, me and her niece

who inherited her property by her will.
After we found the mouse dead,
 them creaking boards became
 as silent as death.
Her niece said she was surprised
we fed it. It was quite unnecessary
because it was only a mouse.
But after the tragedy it made me think."
—

"And what did it make you think,
Lily?" I asked smiling.
The old woman scratched her bun
harpooned by a big bead-headed hairpin
while, we waited for the grandfather clock
in the hall to strike its booming
long drawn out soundings of noon.
—

In the silence she replied:
"I thought maybe Lady Thorndike
might be right. we are all animals,
aren't we, sir? So I suppose we all
 need feeding, don't we?"
"Precisely, Lily! Even mice," I added
 for the benefit of the niece with the
wrinkled prune of a face,
descending the staircase.
—

"The color of compassion
is white, like mice.
Children don't destroy them
with excruciating poison.

Instead, they enjoy
giving them a happy life
with no regrets as pets.
Surely that says enough to us
—why do we have to grow up?"

Cucumber-young

What power had charged our green salad days
that effervesced in Love's erotic dielectric betwixt
the lettuce-fresh and cucumber-young to which
we butterfly lovers so long belonged, mistaking
the hot mustard cress of seductive tongue
and fiery glow of libido for the swan's faithful
ethereal mating and nesting bond. But maybe
it was akin when sighting through Youth's bemused
tinted telescope and viewing as in a rose kaleidoscope
the mirage of enchanted might-have-been. What else
in life has excelled to this extent the body beautiful
and unadorned as a lily beneath our mesmeric gaze?
The sky was never half as bright as by candlelight
and the wondrous magic stars in smiling eyes.
—

The days seemed an unwakable dream until
one sad glance into a cruel glass revealed
that Time our brows, cheeks and necks had ploughed
and at threshold of tired eyes—with the aid of shady
violets—hanging on to the skirts of an Indian summer.
—

Abruptly, the clock had overturned youth's whipped
spinning humming top that spun to a tumbling
standstill. And where had all the music gone?
Crept upstairs like an arthritic snail to sleep
in our bed of memories. Waltzes unburied begin
to lilt—jilted wallflowers wilt, waiting
for that last chance of a dance that will never be asked.
—

By untinted telescope how can we compare the truth
that followed with the glib we swallowed for a tryst in
    the mist?
We weep for the dream we can never retrieve. If only
we could and undo our foolish mischief—step back
in Time to where we stood, when things were good
for so long for the fresh cucumber-young, living
and loving by the light of the moon and the lies of the
    tongue!
—

Many a kindred phantom is among the wistful
weathered cucumber-young crying for the moon
while passing through the haunted glass—moth-ridden
ghosts chewing holes in Love's old clothes.
Yet growing old gracefully is graceless and painful
as buzzing the candle flame and singeing with yearning.
—

Time-distant downstream, patched at the sleeves,
unstitched at the seams, dressed in our soul's soiled
secondhand best, our hopes polished to a sunny
smile to beguile a deer or sagging stag
with fawning eyes—we believe to be our only prospects.
—

But no! A star spears our pillows and we awake
cucumber young and lettuce fresh—Pandora's
opened box, our future's treasure chest.

And behold, our star was Venus and the thought she
    shone
into our unrequited hearts: "soon we shall be lovers
    greeting

as rivers meeting and flowing on as a single stream
crystal clear as the rolling pearl of a tear."
—

Age is but Autumn disguised in its death mask
prematurely placed over our younger face,
revealed beneath at last at the Halloween of hearts
—that eternal moment in suspended Time, when eyes
spark eyes that flint our wildest dreams.
—

O elusive ballroom gazelles we loved too well,
tell me not we Fall lovers have not Spring oozing
from the marrow of arthritic bones—but less rampant
    our horns,
less cloven our hooves at the sparkling watering hole!
Let us pop the cork of belated regrets and the
    unforgettable
put to rest. Time transmogrifies Love's horned
Capricorns into failed swans. And now given the thrill
of a last chance in loving arms, we are more feeling
in tampering with glass hearts—so breakable looking
    back
to when once upon a dream the unbelievable was
    believed.

Eden Without Eve

We began as aspiring angels—our hearts in Heaven
carved on Eden's bark, but decreasingly divine
as Cupid's fledgling arrows missed their mark.
When did we cease pretending—burning out the years
of yearning that ended in the season of tears. Love sleeps
with Vanity and walks with a white cane!
I never believed you'd walk out on me one day,
regrettably for reasons sadly unclear, my dear.
Do you recall, as I do, the Golden Delicious you bore
under your blossom, when I handed you over that style
with warning to trespassers, but bull being a
    camouflage?
We passionate imposters fallen from Paradise—we ache
to regain the mirage—the style, Eden, the season
—hankering for that golden apple in its intimate
    blossom!

Dearest, Did You Hear?

In dreams we live
what the heart cannot bear.
Your head moved
though your eyes were dead.
—

The night was missing its moon;
the stars shot out of the night
and a strange black sun was casting
dream shadows of a past
on virgin snow,
purer than the Carmelite nun
clicking her soul's necklace
of midnight pearls
to kiss you into Heaven
by the veil of celibacy.
In the cloistered abbey
of a forsaken broken promise,
I awoke from a prayer
and saw you there
in the luminance of my heart
—like a ballet of sequins translucent
dancing in your tangerine hair.
—

Through the stained windows
of your sainted eyes
saw I Death's kiss of your last breath
only my own can take from me now.
—

The coffin was closed,

yet, dearest, I could see you clearly
through the wreaths
—you were sleeping
so peacefully beneath
the lilies, fragrantly breathing
in their own sleep.
—

My sleeping beauty,
I could see you so clearly
as if the coffin had been open
—saw the freckles
on your so pretty little nose
as straight as a Roman road
—it ran directly through my thoughts
when first I kissed
those tiny sun spots.
while we fed the swans
—and you as faithful, white
soft as any betrothed among.
How we never dreamed in our days
of perpetual dawn, how our swan's nest
so soon would be glazed in a tomb of ice!
—

Outside in the darkness
the shivering trees
were all naked in the park
—a nude army halted on the march
and the purity of your beauty
a snowdrop frozen at its feet.

Outside, the miller of cold clouds

was grinding his white grains.
And as I knelt at your side
the night was glacial
as its gliding swan
cutting its iced lake
of wedding cake,
for Death's marriage
of silence to Paradise.
—

What faint flakes of sound—if any
ghosted from sealed lips
of your beauty
like the trapped fly
sleeping for ever in amber
inside your bosom's pin.
It crossed my mind—if only I
could be that fly to be closer
to you physically,
that I may hold your hand in Heaven.
—

As I knelt entranced
—miracle or mirage,
I saw through the flowers
how that faintest movement
of your breathless lips
the candles swept!
—

O my dearest love, did your minuscule
murmuring I plainly heard infer
the desolate wolf inside me you could hear,
 as if howling at the moon?

Dearest did you hear?
—I smell the lilies as the candles
flicker, but in whose breath of death?
Beloved, stir once more that I be sure
from the candles' flicker fanned by your lips.
O tell me, dearest, did you hear—did you hear?

Admiral Bembo

Sailors since the bottom of the ocean of Time
have turned into gulls and whispering shells.
Admiral Bembo, so the legend tells,
danced the hornpipe on his missing toes.
A cannon in battle and a pistol in love,
like froth off beer to mariner's ears
he blew away, yet is with us still
—his Admiral's whistle shrill in the spindrift
echoes in the fog from his phantom flagship.
Like a ghost in the mist he drifts,
we never sight him, though we hear him
calling to his shipmates shrieking in the wind.

The Olympic Flame of Misconception

We owe to media mythology the triumph of heroics!
Gory was the glory of the torch of Greek Olympics,
carried into mythology by the runners of the media!
A typical sample for example was the boxing bout,
the buckled knuckled clout unrestrained by rules
was a blood bath as unspeakable as the cock pit.
Fair be the foul and foul be the contest to the finish
—featureless features the facial pulp of victory!
Gargoyles for faces gained laurel crown distinction,
the Greek Olympic gold of the contest to extinction.
It was the human bull fight of Ancient Greece,
the victors unrecognizable by their own mothers.
As for the Hellenic sportsmanship, it glorified gore!
Ours is indeed the Age of disbelief!

Valhalla Hill

Often, we walked together like a moving mushroom
hauled by a greyhound in the rain. Now I walk in the
    clouds
in daylight darkness, my beloved gentle giant
having passed away. He towered above others
of his docile breed—his grave is at my feet,
on the forepaw of Valhalla Hill, where revered animals
are finally laid to rest—and to one who loved me
more than himself, I have come to pay my respects.
—

Autumn to her beauty parlor has gone to dye
crinkled gold her green summer hair.
Crisp are my footsteps whispering to the old tired
trees undressing, shivering in their shirt sleeves,
ready for bed among the furry buried.
Oh, how cold the sun shines and the moon
so warm on fond sleepwalking memories
down the hallowed ground of Valhalla Hill!
Its fur ghost's staircase leads to the Necropolis
of pet Afterlife, in terraces—each with its poignant
memorial stone, or grander marble mausoleum.
—

It was years ago in the snow that my David became
Death's lifelong tenant leased to God,
who says He loves all creatures great and small.
So I must take Him at His word, although I have my
    doubts
—His word being so mysterious and subject to miracles.
—

How I remember that awesome December, when first
I looked up at the tombstones climbing those steepest of
   steps,
as if to be close to Heaven, for God to read
  the inscriptions, and be certain that no single paw is
   missing.
—

Sleeping for ever, David lies hereunder,
my innocent graceful hound, fawn in color
meek in demeanor, and with beautiful eyes, lustrous
wide—elongated like a Pharaoh's. Staring they seemed
to be—into your very soul. And heavily he'd lean
against one's legs, as if to share one's warmth.
Who knew him, took to him spontaneously—always it
   was mutual
—in his naturally skeletal frame not a bone was cruel.
—

David's memorial is unpretentious, limited by my bank
manager's patience. I make up for the rest with flowers
watered regularly by tears of remembrance and Heaven's
contribution, when its clouds in passing pay their
   condolences.
The bride-bright daisies Midas-touch
the buttercups, that smile between the weeds,
making the moribund grave a living place.
—

O how I remember the sweet days
of November, when Autumn lets down her golden hair
while silence whispers in the air (of the dead) secrets
left behind to retrieve as unburied treasure.
O happy dog-walking days on a leash

for David to lick his friends with windmill tails,
built to sail the breeze of sniffing greetings!
O noses to savor the sweet aromas of the wayside,
the Burgundy grapes of roseate fire hydrants
in the flourishing vineyards of the urban sidewalks,
open to canine connoisseurs of bouquet-inhaling.
In addition, the seductive attraction of olfactory
      liquefaction
left behind, like scented handkerchiefs of libido
—temptation by flirtation of the fur-fair sex!
—

Yet even saints are prone enemies to clone,
one in particular grafted to David in his tracks
—a certain popeyed Pomeranian short in stature,
fierce in demeanor, glowering from fireball eyes
glazed by volcanic ire, spitting at no matter
what overwhelming power of enemy fire!
Even at David, thrice its size and to whom
   it presented no cataclysmic daunting show of might!

—

David would look down at his would-be challenger
peacefully—easily able to sidestep
all aggressive progressive maneuvers mighty in
      miniature!
Time and again they invulnerably clashed—Olympic
gladiators of the gutter overly unevenly matched,
locked together in mortal combat, until
Pomeranian, exhausted, David leaped to lick
the cold wet olive of a bellicose nose!

—

To every other a brother was my gentle giant,
and to petting hand a leaning welcoming host,
as doubtless he is now, to his confrere animal ghosts
haunting the terraces of hallowed Valhalla Hill.
Hopefully, he has soared, like the lark to Heaven's gate
to lick the hand of Saint Francis waiting
to introduce him to great Gabriel and the lesser angels.
—

I sip the wine that turns to vinegar
and savor the happy days spent together
—David tugging to his vineyards of the sidewalk
—to join his canine special friends and acquaintants,
and in the park to meet new wagging arrivals
wearing fur coats of multifarious sizes,
and colors to fit their disparate body contours,
including David's favorite. As a slim Dalmatian
spotted rocket, he had speed-appeal, and was elegantly
tailored by Nature's leopard skin furrier.
—

One night, soon after David had died,
I called out in the darkness his name, and heard (I swear),
his fleet footsteps, soft as fur on the stairs!
Another time, I awoke, convinced I could smell
in the kitchen his last supper's Holy Grail!
—

One winter, I recall sitting by the timber embers,
mesmerized by the flickering pine smoldering into
    phantoms.
One, I smelled was materializing—not from fir, but fur
—visibly vaporizing, as if he were lying at my fireside!
And at the same time, in my mind, I heard him howl,

as was his wont, when fire engines screamed by!
—

   If only Cerberus, his Alpha star, could foretell
David being well-nourished and groomed,
ready for knocking on the door with pleading paw
—and the Heavenly portal will be opened unto him
by Saint Francis, smiling with sweet accord,
plus his blessing to present my David to the Lord.
—

His word is affirmed by a certain beautiful hymn,
"And His mercies shall endure, ever faithful
ever sure"—most reassuring. Especially, in continuum:
"run the straight race with God's good grace"
—so apposite with a sleek fleet greyhound in mind!
I could imagine my David becoming the hot favorite
of the "straight race" in Heaven's "Grand National,"
and thrilling cheering cherubim, saints and angels!
—

The day is gray, my heart is overcast,
at his grave-side. My thoughts are downcast
to where he lies a fathom below my shadow.
All pious prayers to no avail, Jesus had somehow
failed to raise him, like Lazarus from the dead, when
    David
fell—painfully, and fatally, stricken in the hip.
—

It was a Sunday, and on the tiles he had to remain all
    night,
—sprawling, legs kicking, struggling to rise.
When helped to his feet, he sank forthwith and stayed
crooked in my arms on the floor, helplessly soaking

the rug, for his urinal maypole was hopelessly
    unreachable.
Veterinarians proclaiming to be on call were
    unobtainable
—till the office opened on Monday for business as usual!
Pain pills hopefully relieved, but those
he swallowed repeatedly for sleeping took no affect.
A vet' explained "he was desperate not to be leaving his
    Alpha."
—

On Monday morning, when the office opened, not
    before,
he passed away peacefully, his head in my arms,
and not knowing why a tiny prick like a mosquito
mercifully, suddenly put a dreamy end to his misery.
—

At the foot of Valhalla Hill eternally he sleeps
level with the highway, adjacent to a delicatessen,
convenient for his ghost to haunt the savory smells
my David loved so well. In my mind still
I feel him tethered to my stride, until I realize
with a sudden chill that Time has passed and cruel
Death has come and caught my David by the tail.
—

If only I could see a holy smoke signal
akin to issuing from the Vatican—Heaven's soaring
plume of approval to bless the cap of a cardinal.
I needed to know my David was truly chosen
for his innocence and devotion. Alas! I saw only
smoke—and none more glorious than from the pet
    crematorium.

—
Beneath the raven's wings of night, I dreamed
and joyously perceived a hearse in Heaven. It was carrying
my David to St. Francis to be given, not merely the
     "blessing
of the animals," but his last rites, the passport to
     Paradise.
"The straight race" he obviously had won—and his
     reward.
Now, my pensive eyes are glazing upon
the wilted flowers and weeds waltzing in the breeze.
I am waiting to freeze to his howling, as a fire engine
comes screaming by as if from very Hell!

—

I wait and wait in vain—upwards I creep
—a fragile penurious snail, to pay my fees
to the parlor for top quality quilted casket,
assumed preeminently suited to making David's
deserved debut into the very highest society.

—

However, so meager my sepulcher compared with the
     wonder,
grandeur and splendor of the Taj Mahal, that touching
Indian potentate's elephantine tribute weighed
in gold, ivory and pearls. His mausoleum's towering
tiered wedding cake, iced with marble
immortalized a marriage made in Heaven and lost
in Paradise below where mortals die. How puny
my unpretentious slab miserably compared, weighed
for judgment, in peanuts, tears and tacit prayers!

—

I passed the impressive tomb of a Teutonic hound
of Heaven to the manor born to die. "Here
lies my beloved Daxie. I named him Prince,
because to me, he was greater than the great Dane!"
   The marble showpiece in memoriam of that royal
      appellation
was crumbling, cut down by Time's decay,
its mourner whisked away by the scythe of Religion
to a distant graveyard where pets are frowned upon.
Did Heaven care how inseparable the parted pair?
—

I can hear the spade, somewhere lower in the hierarchy
of terraces, where bones are graded by fees received,
while only wealth may touch the hem of Heaven.
The gravedigger was singing the psalm of the gaping soil
for a new arrival for the survival of the voracious worms
—a haunting companion for David—a snowball of a St.
      Bernard,
Switzerland's sainted animal, for Valhalla's alp.
—

Nostalgia will never evaporate the looking down
on the beloved face of my departed greyhound David,
not gray, but fair as a frolicsome young fawn,
in sleep awake and dewy as the dawn. In a dream
he seemed to be, smiling through a window at the world.
True to death was the pet cemetery's chapel,
with its altar candles flickering shadows on the corpse's
catafalque—softening my negative introspection upon
      those
who protest that no animal possesses the profundity of
      a soul.

But gazing into the gloaming of a dog's eyes, how
could we doubt that deep in their depths, the denied
    resides?
—
I glance at my watch, the gates are due to close.
Heavenward I peer to the moonlit summit—now
mist and crystal grist from the mills of God,
grinding His snowy flour by sails ever turning.
Suddenly, the cemetery is a sleeping beauty beneath
 her train of vestal veils, gradually draping
the terraces, tumbling in a hillside cascade of revered
fur interred and breathless bones. O the ineffable
coalescence of his presence, as suddenly, the scene
    turned
awesomely wild. Lightning kept striking, a fire
engine screamed. And straining my ears, I could hear
his desolate eerie wolflike howl! But from such great
distance—not certain heard entirely in my ears
—not by echo of that familiar physical feeling of leaning
on my legs—and if not legs, then solely against my own
    soul!
Thereupon, rang the gates, and clanged with such
    finality!

Footprints in the Fog

Here I, Poetry's purblind missing person,
returned from the brine having "swallowed the anchor"
    in harbor
of obloquy (an unintended soliloquy)! This sailor
    dolphin,
was he merely dreaming he had performed in spectacular
    fashion
—leaped through the rainbow of hope of being noticed,
and earning applause? Is it poetic justice that the missing
person be missing an audience—gone to the aquarium
where unremarkable guppies blow bubbles
through the glass? Van Gogh, Art's sunflower,
now the richest corpse in history, sold
but one petal of his life's bouquet. And History
is the parrot of itself. So with salt thrown
over my shoulder and my guide dog's paws
crossed, may my footprints be amber in the fog.

Love in Winter is Summer in Disguise

If love were a tree, its blossom you would be
while I a bird therein its fragrance would sing.
If love were the sun, its rays would ripen the cherries
of your breasts, the sheaves of your hair, and I in heaven
harvesting there, gathering the grain for ever
and a day and by night stow away in my heart.
If love were those passing clouds, they would rain
on my mountain side. Even so, the highest
summits our hopes can climb cannot eclipse
 the stars in eyes when they smile. Love is the fantasy
creating the ecstasy when eyes beguile. Nothing
 that lips can say the heart cannot deny.
Although there exists no absolute truth, yet heartfelt
 proof that love in winter is summer in disguise.

Down the Crooked Path

Hung by the strings of Faith we human puppets
—dangling to the dance, walk the crooked path
of life on the boards by the hidden Power
    choreographed.
When fallen by the wayside—dropped upon our
    faces,
we fated thespians of theocracy, let us feel no disgrace
dancing to controlling fingers fouling our strings.
If sin we inherit and it is the price of puppets to pay,
marionettes swinging in the dark, be never dismayed
by false prophets in the lofty critical boxes
taking joy from our performance by slow clapping
our naked happening on stage. A bullion of bliss
is measurable in the corporal flesh, not credit of the
    spirit!
Yet Paradise if granted the gift of belief—when our
    starlight
show is over and the ground is hollow for dropping
earth on our loved ones, faithful shadows may follow.

Artemis in Acapulco

Limbs were splayed
on the burning sand,
the sensitive toasting
lobster red
—others skinning like a snake,
piebald pink
as the ghost of a shrimp
—and the glamorous glowing bronze.
Flies were defying
flying hand
aerosol and parasol.
Childhood was dipping
its croissants of diapers
straggling bowlegged legs
in the foaming mouths
of Neptune's white horses,
that youth uncouth was riding,
while newspaper was shading
its sleeping fireball of a face.
—

Along the crunching shingle
the children's lollipop angel
alighted creaking
on arthritic wings.
The tide's cool barber lisping
was busy lathering limbs
soaking in the whiskery shrimps'
shaving water.
A minuscule gladiator,

bucket for helmet,
spade for lance,
locked in mortal combat
with a lion of little dog
wagging its windmill tail
—another chasing
the ghost of a crab
vanishing through a weedy rock.
It was a day for pursuing leisure
digging for treasure
among the buried memories.
—

And a shrieking choir
of Heaven's mendicant friars
on the Feast of Saint Francis
from their cloudy cloisters
swooped upon our consciences
with their begging beaks.

And through the surreal
ethereal kaleidoscope
a young dream floated,
alighting onto the sand
to seed in my mind.
Soon she was a flower
behind a tortoiseshell butterfly
settling onto her pretty nose.
She filters fantasies
through fairest eyes
that match the sky
when all its sheep have died.

—
The mold for that beautiful body
was waiting for hot sunlight
to cast her youth in all its
loveliness, in living bronze
—the beet of her lips,
the wheat of her hair,
  the ripening corms of her breasts.
  Beside her I lay chewing an ancient
 legend in my introspection,
  while the moon of Artemis
  projected her radiance,
  by the will of Zeus,
  with the blessing of Apollo
  pouring his molten sister
  from the furnace-glow
  of Acapulco into a mold
  of the virgin goddess
—cooling and cast (as I awoke)
  into the breathing bronze of a girl.

A Salt Water Mystery

Glorious as the sun was shining,
myself on the beach reclining
—distinctly I heard
a female voice,
but the beach was a forsaken desert
except for the crabs
and hungry gulls scavenging.
My eye fell
upon a lone vacated shell
—and putting it to my ear
could faintly hear
a poor woman
sobbing to my throbbing heart.

I was not mistaken,
it was not the wind haunting
from a crustacean coffin,
or simply a ghost of my imagination.

Long I listened enthralled
and above all
two salt tears
fell convincingly
warm on my naked knee.

Years later at sea
an old seaman
explained the occult mystery
—and not through his beard!

For his mind was clean-shaven
and sharp as a bos'n's whistle.
Our ship was rolling to the main,
like a porpoise with a bellyache,
and we both clammed
for dear life to the rail.

His eyes drifted
on the ebb of a thought
and when he spoke
it was as if Time was listening
through a telescope
to truths transparent
and ancient as jellyfish.

"That sobbing you heard in a shell
be the captain's spirit,
them gulls was not scavenging
but communicating!
Them tears wot dropped was real."

He paused for the mercury
of the meaning in the barometer
of my mind to fall,
then proceeded dead ahead,
after I had said:
"But I heard a woman sobbing?"
"Naturally! Because it wa his widow!"

Sleeping Dolphin

In a green-green glade of Glamorgan, the wet jewel
of the mountains, that weeping emerald—a sailor was
    born
again like a sleeping dolphin awakening. Oh, he rode
his unsinkable cork of a girl on the white horses
of devotion! But now he kneels to his queen, crowned
in the clouds. As a shadow floats the ocean, he follows
as faithfully as the fated bird of the Ancient Mariner,
yet he dreams content in the wake of loving spent
—an albatross of memories shot down in his bunk.
She fled on their tide at its solstice, fresh as spindrift,
and from his drowned nemeses the gull flies as its spirit,
while never bled pain like the soul without veins.
Lost Love is the sonar of sorrow—the tears
of a dreaming dolphin sounding saline into the brine.

Barking to the Heart

Barking to the heart
from behind bars,
puppies rescued
fluffy and cuddly
or grizzly and scruffy,
in the Samaritan Daycare
of animal welfare
—pitiable pendulums of tails
to hypnotize the adoptive eye.
Each pup or mature mutt,
handsome or plain,
is keeping paws crossed to be
the chosen dog of our dreams!
Yet every arrested wanderer
picked up from the streets
—lap size or jumbo junior,
needing to be needed,
is an incarcerated innocent
on canine Death Row,
waiting for reprieve.
—

And as we fade from sight
utter despair we overhear,
as the last bark in our ears
as we go out the door.
—

But If you take a dog
with pity in your heart,
you have found

the only friend
you will ever know
who truly loves you
even more than himself.

Only Love Can Hold a Candle to the Moon

Often I wilt, conscience creaks and to bed
I creep like a wounded mouse afraid to tread.
I hear the sprung trap snap in the night
and excruciating the cheese! It has broken the back
of our love. Solace I seek with the fairies at the foot
of the staircase at the bottom of my mind. As I listen,
kindly they whisper inside my heart: "Love
is overlooking our imperfections—Life
is not growing roses—the soil is quicklime. Our petals
drop in the withering heat of gospel and parable.
Love is not seasonal under the glasshouse of our faults
although the holier-than-thous may throw stones.
Only Love can hold a candle to the moon,
for Life is a glass heart sinning in the dark.

Whispers into Darkness

As I blindly turn the pages of my raised brail
of introspection, I feel her beloved face
like a peaceful lily lying on the lake of night.
I detect the soft throbbing of her heart, like the flight
of a wispy dragonfly humming in the moonlight.
Although she has flown to unknown pastures, long ago,
yet do I hear her near, as if breathing on my pillow
—soft as a mosquito sleeping on dark water.
In summer, I can decipher the secret code of fireflies
signaling in sparks to their lovers replying from the
    grass.
Inspired by the faint ethereal flinted luminosity
a spark from the heart can soar to a star—how
    otherwise,
could so keenly I *feel* her beauty somewhere about
mystically gravitating to be close in the abysmal
    blackout?

Apollo in a Pink Mirror

Love is the mystic fairytale of wishful thinking.
Though the fantasy of a raven preening in the dark,
Vanity paints Beauty vanishing into glass.
But in a shaving mirror, who cuts under the lather?
For although the surface be, superficially, skin deep,
yet profounder than the ocean—so reflects the heart at eye
level. In the mysterious mirage of ephemeral Life,
cursed are we with princes blessed. Cinderella
wept, for never from saddle His Highness swept!
Gretel not sweeter than chocolate—nor Hansel
    handsomer
than Grimm! Foolishly, we parted with our carte blanche
to the Queen of Diamonds, passing it on to the Knave of
    Hearts.
The brightest beautiful fairytale is Love, like the sun
when begun, and dying as Apollo turning into a swan.

Death of a Smile

By the faint glimmer of my ailing glowworm of sight,
never to silver shall turn the gold of her hair
as the worsening weather of Time tarnishes the years,
for the feet of crows vanish in my starless night.
Timelessly she passes through Beauty's hourglass,
as the glorious mirage of the ageless desert sand.
In my melon moon of fantasy—a melting slice
of our youth to savor in the Arctic of my frozen sun.
Through the wasp-waist of the days' dripping grains
she is gone, yet with me, for I feel her haunting still
as phantom silhouettes in my fog that never lifts
—our talking shadows as specters on a blind.
Till I am no more, I shall see her in my vision's hoar
evermore as my summer in winter's everlasting flower.

In Another Life

As I lay dreaming in my lonely bed,
Time's following albatross
is swooping onto my clouded head
of a very distant Past drifting through
the swirling mists. The sun shines
through the fog of gaslight moon
and at noon woke the sky in your eyes,
while about me your hair flew the air
as the raven of night.
How can I ever forget you
who were my very wife
long ago in another life?
—
How beautiful you looked
in your bustle whispering silk!
The wasp of your waist stung my hand
around when we sat feeding the swans
long in the neck as our arms—reminisces
we sipped lip unto lip, kisses betwixt.
—
The night has lost its tide, forgotten, abandoned
by the moon melting like butter in the dish of summer.
We watch the white-feathered ghosts gliding
trailing their smoke of shadows
dissolving into darkness in the park.
The yawn of dawn approaching,
awakens the heavenly lark,
while our albatross returning
nests in my captive heart.

—
Time hallucinates—places, fond faces
out of sequence to events as we peer
lit by the bright sequins of night,
but in our opaque water looking-glass,
Gladiesa, your beloved face I see always last.
And when like a stream deluges the rain
and the wind trembles in the ague
of window panes, I *feel*
your presence in my very veins!
—
Time's fated ocean bird follows
our phantom ship of dreams
bourne on a zephyr that makes
the fleet of trees sail their crisp
autumnal seas of leaves.
Ecstatic I hear the electric
whispering silk of my faithful beloved
wife locked in an erstwhile life!
—
A surreal mist descends and in a mysterious
mistral, Past and Present blend
in light transcending its spectrum.
—
O beloved, baroness-with-a-broom
—I kissed you in the kitchen
and you swept me off my feet
from this life into the twilight
beside your coffin in the clouds.
I was euphoric. At that instant
if you had been an angel and I a saint

I could not have loved you more, nor
have been more bewitched had you ridden
like a witch, your menial's sweeping switch!
—

We peeled our youth squeezing out the juice
as if the fruitful season would outlast its mood.
O Gladiesa, baroness-with-a-broom,
our lives were intertwined, when you took over
from your servants, as traditional reversal of behavior.
It is uncanny, I hear your hissing globes of gaslight
when I turn on our silent bulbs of frosted glass.
—

O Gladiesa how could I have known
that I would be the cause
—and the Dark Angel of the eternal tide
cleave you from me, mother and child-bride?
Déjà vu is Love's illusionist of departed illusions,
nothing is more real than the fantasy
to those who live the ecstasy,
and doomed to dream beyond
the sleep as you and I, my dear.
O my flower, I can smell your perfume
—and the reason is becoming poignantly clear.
—

Menials in mourning—like the black pieces
of a chess board—all waiting for the
next move, myself included most subdued
—callabra scintillating the catafalque, simulating
an altar—its offering to Eternity the facsimile
of a china doll in her pram waiting
to be pushed to Paradise by a mother child.

O Gladiesa, she is none other
than you by *déjà vu!*
—

All the while I cried, my grief falling upon
the sunset painted onto your cheeks, as if my tears
were your very own, and you were weeping in your sleep.
Your lips are death's blue ice by the parlor dyed red
—an awesome reminder as to which side of the abyss
I have fled and am dreaming from. No cave was ever
lonelier or deeper than my bottomless grief.
—

The coffin is as formal as teacakes
of Viennese delicacy, from the oven
of a master mortician pastry cook
of rigor mortis, who skillfully concealed
every vestige of aging. So you resemble
in your coffin, less the diminutive
child-mother than her rosebud china child.
And although you were not a practicing Catholic,
the parlor in its fervor to curry favor, had strung
papal beads through your fingers, furthermore
flung death from your beloved face
by dyeing its labial blueberries red.
But the dewy bluebells of your eyes
so ethereal, I would not allow to be closed,
for even in everlasting rest I wanted you to be able
to look me in the eyes and know that their loving gaze
gives back to you your own for evermore. As I stare
you appear so lifelike, one could not be certain
those pale curtains undrawn did not restrain
the faintest vestige of a living blink!

—
O my beloved Gladiesa, how you starlight
my inspiration as I paint
your incomparable nude portrait in the air
by the glowworm of a star in my heart.
Do not stir, beloved, keep perfectly still
a little longer in my *déjà vu,* to give me time
to paint you immaculately immortalized.
Keep as still as the marble angel on your tomb.
Love transcends the planting of Death
in the graveyard soil. O Gladiesa! you seem
to be breathing and sprouting mystically grafted
like an orchid into my afterlife—nearer and nearer
I feel you approach until I smell your sweet breath
mingling with mine. How then can you be in Heaven
as mistakenly inscribed upon your sepulcher? O
    Gladiesa!
I can taste on my lips your own. Oh, so imperceptibly as
    ghosts
—so we must have kissed! As if to keep awake
the night is drinking our black Viennese fig
flavored coffee. And I can smell your perfume redolent
as ever, as if we were sitting together—and yet
two centipedes of years have crept and I still remember
as if both had only one leg! I see the sparks
from our carriage wheels drawn by your white-plumed-
horses in our gaslight old Vienna streets,
where the ivy of our memories clings and sings
    happiness.
—My heart leaps each time I hear your stallions neighing.
The coachman opens the carriage door and delicately

you step down like a fairy princess to the ball
—in glass slippers to break my glass heart.
Life was a *"pas de deux de plaisir d'amour!"*
as your French chaperone reported to our bitter cost,
while if she had not, we would never have eloped
and you, dearest, would never have been my child-bride.
How Fate, not we decided our own unchosen.
—

Dearest, how I felt the raven of your tresses
perching upon my shoulders as I lay looking up
at Heaven in the azure of your eyes.
And, my dearest sweetest angel, from that unearthly
angle I remember ringing the bell of your hovering
bustle over my spider-fingers climbing
the slender silken ladder of your fabulous legs,
while your laugher pealed in pearls as a rosary
for my latter-day lips to kiss beyond the abyss.
O my sleeping beauty, to the echo of a song
in my heart you shall always in the twilight belong
to the flower of our everlasting summer.
—

Dearest love, the night is fluttering its wings,
did you not hear the leaves in the breeze embracing
down the paths we trod, and my trembling
living ghost in the dark whistling?
—

Our swans in the park were white hopes begging
while a hand in the night—not mine, fed them bread
—yours it must have been? If you cannot speak,
can you faintly move your head instead?
Or if silence can be the word, let it be said.

—
O Gladiesa, keep close to me
as we travel together through memory
for ever and ever—lost souls in the dark
crying out to our hearts. Ever the scene changes
—Vienna by the lake feeding the swans,
in your castle kitchen where love began
to the ballroom in splendor, where the Danube whose
silken ribbon under the sequins of Heaven ran,
with you sleeping like a lovely lily
on the white water of your lake of beauty
in the chapel under the flickering candles
and flowers. O beloved angel-wife-
in-another-life, I know you will never leave me
because you are only oversleeping.
Looking into the mirror of Danube water, I see
our sweet selves kissing. Gladiesa, angel-mine,
I take comfort in hearing you whisper: "In the garden
of our souls immortal roses grow, while in the orchard
of our longing, Love is to each other the belonging,
the ecstasy, Life the fantasy, its fruit the expectancy,
ever ripe and chaste to taste. Beyond the abyss
what is love but a dissolving dream? To what
does the dreamer awake into but the living dream?
We have each other, what does it matter
which side of the border
—when one life is over, begins another?"

Sleeping Swan

In the eider of your eternal nest your beauty stirs
in the breathless sleep you left behind in my mind.
O let's go out to feed the hungry gulls
and feel their shrieking glee as they fall from a cloud.
How can it be, your lips are still ripest raspberries,
your blue eyes open as the cloudless sky
staring as if loth to let me out of your sight?
How could my guardian angel permit the bloom
of innocence to blow in summer and not wait till winter?
Are they so short of angels in Heaven that they need
to steal them from here?" "O what stupid questions!"
I can hear you saying in your sleep. True, you always
had right answers to questions and I the wrong to ask
O swan of my life, I cannot live without your answers!

Paws in Paradise

God, if you in all mercy exist,
please give me the gift
of faith in the power of prayer,
that I may visit Heaven
hopefully to find my Coco there,
winged white and wonderful,
begging from Saint Francis
at the Lord's table
—and barking at the glorious angels.
O God if your mercies do endure
be sure to grant me the air ticket
at your golden gate to show,
that I may visit my Coco
and be with you both a day or two.
For she and kind Saint Francis
in all mercy must agree,
on bended knee I need to plead
for what it is worth to return to earth.
Because we who imagine ourselves
so great have stolen from the small,
who now desperately deserve all
the help they should receive
in struggling in our world to feed themselves.

Cat Worship
(Dedicated to fellow seamen)

To Neptune's idolatrous
sharp card playing
nicotine-stained sea cook,
the galley cat is a god,
the very ace of "spades"
shuffled from a ship's pack
black fur backed,
and bringing an ocean of luck
to its superstitious worshipers.
They include the captain, of course,
right down to the able-bodied
and disabled three sheets
in the wind on a Force Nine,
scuppers in the brine.
Plus the flea on watch
on the cat's sta'b'd whisker
and hopping along that yard
to be hung by its own petard
—ringing the feline ship's bell
(by its "Turk's head)"
—while the big brass thing
is "catted" to the deckhead
of the great god cat's neck.

The Older We Grow

We live in the sun and love in the passing clouds.
We grow wings in our dreams, then folly usually follows
for we grow older and no wiser it seems, as the mistaken
sages of ageing. The virtuous and the unchaste taste
in the black bowl of the stars the heart's spoiled fruits
of sorrow. And on the morrow, we stick to our faults like
    flies
hanging from their lofty gallows of glutinous demise.
In the orchard of Love we keep picking the fallen!
The older we grow the grayer we go, the less
like rabbits of habit, more like dusty owls
hooting ignorance from our lonesome boughs.
We weather our feathers with diminishing grace. Sadly
we grow slower, nearer Heaven but seldom heavenlier.
Time grows moss and sets our earthly pace to the grave.
Walking mushrooms follow in the rain dripping their
    affection,
disenchantment or indifference, in willows or crocodile
    tears.
Through our mother's tunnel of love we squeeze
and smack into life loud as the dawn chorus.
Ultimately, silently and reluctantly, mostly, we depart
as a mole of Faith in its tunnel blocking the light.

Shipwrecked Mariners of the Heart

How can we drop anchor
in heavy seas of rancor?
We steer by the wind on our necks
but not knowing if to reef or gybe.
Shall it be plain sailing on the tide
or beam ends in the brine?
Are we on course by false stars,
we mariners without charts?
From deck to crow's nest
it's just anybody's guess.
Nobody truly knows
until the ship rolls over.
Mercurial is the glass,
while every other lover
is a fair weather sailor
when the wind blows hard.

The River of Love

The river of Love is as fresh as a running spring,
longer than Life, wider than the miraculous Sea
of Galilee, swifter than a gull soaring out of sight,
profounder than any thought in the greatest mind.
And in love we are all phantoms in that heavenly mist,
vanishing as crystal dewdrops on the windows of our
    souls.
In Love's blindness I tap in the fog, for I am one
whose feet don't touch the ground, cannot swim,
cannot fly, but can walk, while I keep looking,
looking across the river to where Love resides
—looking, looking. And what am I doing besides
looking like a fool? I will tell you my secret: why
I've not made it across—I cannot swim but oh, can walk!
I can almost walk on water. I'm just waiting for a miracle.

His Master's Voice

The dead larks sang plaintively
from a flat black wax planet
orbiting its moon of metal horn,
while its haunting voices
thrilled us to the core.
Ghosts materialized revolving
twelve-inch disks of hissing wax
worn smooth in their groves
and scratched out of track.
The dead larks injected
by the needle, galvanized
the beautiful songbirds back to life
—mysteriously through the spirit horn.
—

A listening seance began with the medium
calling from a cloud out of sight.
Through the cosmic static of needle scratching
those long dead larks of bygone Fate
were recalled to sing at heaven's gate.
Time's anomalous sound barrier broken,
their voices carried passing through
the vales of echoing sonic heartbreak
in the whispering caves of spatial
unrequited love transcendent
—held up to ransom
and waiting for those relating
most heavenly of notes to resonate.
—

Fritz Kreisler's voice had four strings

and he bowed them till they bore
their renowned unique rich chords
—dedicated to his little white terrier
listening entranced while chasing his tail
as the wax circle circled blurring
 the revered canine image
 into seventy-five revolutions
of immortalized hermetic sound.
All cranked into being by the unseeing,
plus tedium of tiring hands
guided by invisible medium
—like a phantom out of hearing,
in some unknown sky
—calling the spirits to the horn.

"Come in Fritz Kreisler, bring
your violin tucked under your arm
—come in, Aussie prima donna
Dame Nellie Melba,
come from down-under
and warble velvety like a peach!"
—
A new medium has taken over,
the spirit horn—reborn
as laser's lazy self-propelling
sonic singing shell.
Yet after the facelift
the house is haunted still.
Nostalgically and hypnotically,
by swing of the ticking metronome
gnostic minds are swung to deep sleep

and smoldering memories of the little white dog
somewhere out there lost in the ineffable fog
—and now sniffing the air for his master's voice.

Child of Heaven

In a green green glade in Glamorgan,
Time smiled in those laughing days
when she was my little Bo-Peep
and I her little Boy Blue.
A sheep was asleep in her eyes,
while her ponytail was willow yellow
as the dangling yellow-green by our stream.

In that green green glade of Glamorgan,
it was always top of the morning,
miming our romantic elders
till the cows went home to tea.
A knot tied I in her ponytail
just like in a fairytale
—for love, the cow mooed
while grunted the pig, too,
who could tell that the knot
was so hot it melted the buttercups.

In a green green glade of Glamorgan,
our grasshopper days have hopped away.
The willow still drinks from the cup of her stream,
where a sheep fell asleep in her eyes
in the love that passed us by
—for now our cow has jumped over the moon.

For we mooing-meadow larks in Glamorgan,
the sun spun fun on its fancy loom
for cobweb clouds, while the daisies shone

sunny side up to light the buttercups.
O if only Time was too busy to fly away,
I'd tie a forget-me-not in Bo-Peep's ponytail.

Shadow

Sleepwalking through the window, a moonlit phantom
whispered: "I'm your shadow, I shall thee follow."
I awoke and spoke: "O true ghost, why do you?"
"Because I love you," answered my faithful shadow,
"I follow thee everywhere." I inquired: "When I quit this
    life,
Will you follow me still?" "Indeed I will," assured
the clinging fly of a wraith—it now kneeling on the
    ceiling.
The grandfather clock tolled from its tower below,
calling the hours to prayers. I asked of the ghost
(beginning curling like smoke) above my bed: "Do you
    pray
for my soul?" And it shook its darkness negatively. "But
    surely
you believe?" I exclaimed, "Don't tell me we pray in vain
—there has to be a Heaven?" The specter, as it vanished
    sighed:
 "Not to my knowledge—but until we arrive we never
    can tell."

About the Author

Dr. Jonathan Russell is a poet, an educator, an author, and a composer. He holds an Honorary Doctorate of Literature, London Institute for Applied Research (London, 1993) and Docteur des Lettres, Psychologie et Litterature, Academie Des Sciences Humaines Universelles (Paris, 1993). He is an Honorary Professor of Humanities at the Institute of Higher Economic and Social Studies in Brussels, Belgium. Russell was chosen as "International Literary Man of the Year for Services to Poetry," in 1995 by the International Biographical Center of Cambridge. He received the grand prize in 1998 and again in 1999 from the American Poetry Association and he has been admitted to the Academy of American Poets.

Dr. Russell collaborated with Russian folk singer Sasha Rosenbaum on a peace song for Gorbachev, which was sung at the White House during the signing of the peace treaty by President Bush Sr. He has performed extensively on BBC Radio, and on Long Island, NY television. Dr. Russell is a resident of Port Chester, New York, near New York City.

www.ingramcontent.com/pod-product-compliance
Lightning Source LLC
Chambersburg PA
CBHW051756040426
42446CB00007B/400